CLOSING
TACTICS

OTHER BOOKS BY THE AUTHOR

1st Impressions: How to Greet and
Qualify for Effective Sales

The 10 Cornerstones of Selling: How to
Develop an Effective & Powerful Selling Style

CLOSING TACTICS

HOW TO USE FAST AND EFFECTIVE CLOSING TECHNIQUES

Andoni Lizardy

Amsterdam • Johannesburg • London
San Diego • Sydney • Toronto

Interior Designer: Nicola Ruskin
Cover: Tom Lewis, Inc.

Pfeiffer & Company
8517 Production Avenue
San Diego, CA 92121-2280

ISBN: 0-89384-235-4 (previous ISBN 0-932238-61-0)

Printed in the United States of America
Printing 1 2 3 4 5 6 7 8 9 10

DEDICATION

This book is dedicated to my friend, Sam K. Roy, who practices the art of closing on nearly every continent in this world. May your good works speak for you.

This book is also dedicated to the thousands of people who have been my students, and especially to those students who have enhanced my knowledge of communicating, closing, and selling.

My Special Thanks...
to Kathleen Webber, Teena Eber, Rita Hoepp, and Linnea Dayton, who have contributed greatly to this book. Their exceptional assistance, charm, and wit made the writing of this book a joyful experience.

CONTENTS

TABLES

INTRODUCTION

This is the right book for you if you are searching for ways to improve your closing skills.

This book offers twenty-three proven professional closing techniques. Rarely, if ever, are salespeople formally taught these skills. Few *closing* books or sales managers ever break down the closing process in a simple and clear way with such a large variety of closing examples (over two hundred closing variations and combinations of the original twenty-three categories). This work is therefore unique in that it teaches closing in a logical way.

Closing Tactics can help improve your closing skills and minimize the amount of effort and time invested in the process. It can help you close more transactions more professionally and more often. It shows various ways to bring closure to your presentation. You will discover

- Who should initiate the closing process.
- What to do when a customer rejects your close.
- Where closing mistakes occur and how to avoid them.
- When to initiate a close and when to avoid using a close.
- Why the Ten Laws of Closing are critical to your success.

Plus, you will learn how to

- Develop your closing skills.
- Implement a variety of closes.
- Use low-risk closes successfully.

While *Closing Tactics* is designed for sales, marketing, and customer-service people, it is also written for any person who wants to become

1. A better closer.
2. A more effective negotiator.
3. A more persuasive communicator.
4. A more productive sales or customer-contact person.

If you are a sales manager, I suggest you purchase a copy of this book for each of your people. If you are a business owner or manager, I suggest you purchase a copy for every person involved in customer service, credit, collections, inside sales, marketing, public relations, and customer contact. Someday this small investment will bring or save you or your organization a major account.

This small book offers a large amount of information. For best results, read it carefully. If you skim read, picking up a few ideas here and there, you will extend the time it takes to develop your closing skills. But if you read it carefully, study, analyze, and practice the techniques offered herein, you will profit greatly.

For those of you who may be interested in reviewing the steps of the sale that precede the close, I suggest reading my book *1st Impressions*.

A special thank you for your interest. Good reading and good closing.

Best wishes,

Andoni Lizardy

1

CLOSING TACTICS

Purpose, Objectives, How and When to Close

A close is a statement of agreement
between a buyer and a seller.

"I'm not a good closer," the salesperson advised as I slipped the videocassette of his roleplay into the playback machine. "As a matter of fact, I've spent most of my business career in customer service. Selling is still rather new to me."

"Don't worry," I reassured him. "I'm sure you did better during this roleplay than you might expect."

I was right. For the next few minutes we watched the salesperson roleplay in a selling situation with a fellow employee.

"The customer is giving you a buying signal," I mentioned as the videotape played on. "You didn't respond to his interest in your services."

"That wasn't very good, was it?" he asked shyly.

I stopped the tape.

"It could have been better. The important thing is that you understand that he was searching for more information, which gave you an opportunity to answer his question and attempt a trial close."

"Trial close?"

"Yes. A trial close is a subtle question that allows you to seek the customer's agreement without jeopardizing your transaction."

He was one of the more conscientious members of the class. He took notes, asked good questions, and was interested in improving his selling style. He was also struggling with the basic rules that guide salespeople through the closing process.

"Did you hear the buying signal?" I asked.

"I heard it on the playback but not during the role-play."

"You sound like a typical salesperson," I teased.

"That bad?" he teased back.

"Forget the word *bad*. We all make mistakes. The idea here is to spot the mistake and learn from it. Let's avoid unnecessary criticism and get on with reviewing your roleplay. You showed a great deal of sincere interest in the prospect's needs. That's a plus in any selling situation. It's obvious that he liked the way you responded to his questions. Since you had such a good rapport with the customer, did you attempt to seek an agreement for an order?"

"Yes, I did. We stopped the tape just short of my first closing attempt," he answered.

His last comment was an understatement, for within the next seven minutes of his roleplay the salesperson asked the customer thirty-six different questions, including a large number of trial closes.

"Excellent!" I shouted when the tape ended. "Your questions were relevant, asked in a positive and supporting way, and your customer was comfortable with your approach."

"But I didn't get the order," he insisted.

"I know. Don't worry about the close. Your roleplaying partner was told not to make a purchase no matter how well you performed. The idea here was to test your abilities, persistence, and professionalism."

"Thank you, but I don't understand what I did that was so right."

"You asked the customer important questions. Without gathering that information you would never have been able to address his needs, make your presentation, or close effectively."

"Yes, but they were commonsense questions."

"Correct. You asked relevant questions in a logical sequence."

He paused, and then asked, "But doesn't everyone do that?"

"Hardly. After watching thousands of selling roleplays by both experienced and novice salespeople, I would have to say that most sellers don't plan out their questions well, even after they've been given instructions on how and what to ask."

"Well, the instructions that preceded the roleplay helped a lot."

"Good. Now stick to those instructions when you get back to the real selling world. Do you realize that you asked thirty-six questions in less than seven minutes?"

"No. It just seemed natural to do so. Since my prospect was so open to offering me information, I asked as many questions as possible."

"That's right—what made your questions so effective was that the process was natural. It was so natural that you slipped right into a number of closing questions and the customer didn't even seem aware that the process was taking place."

This salesperson is like thousands of other salespeople my associates and I have trained over the past twenty years. He was unaware of his mistakes as they were occurring. Yet, on the playback he noticed his errors without prompting. He was also unaware of the positive things he was doing. What seemed like common sense to him is often overlooked by even experienced salespeople. His logical approach to the selling process was most effective, and yet he confessed that he was not a consistently successful closer.

His closing challenges are ones that many share, for instance:

- A lack of conscious awareness of how to close effectively and consistently.
- A lack of instruction regarding how to close and a lack of roleplaying experience.
- A lack of knowledge dealing with how to monitor oneself during the selling process.
- A lack of training in how to respond to a prospect's objections and rejection of closes.

Perhaps nothing is more frustrating to a salesperson than the inability to close a prospect. This book was written specifically for those who want to overcome this challenge. Any singular reference to sales is made for the sake of brevity and is intended to include customer-contact people and all who desire to improve their closing skills.

Since this book covers in detail the fifth step of the sale (the close), it can help you gain a greater conscious understanding of how to reach agreements with others. The close is preceded by four other steps, as noted in Table 1-1.

Table 1-1 The Anatomy of the Sale
Summary of the Five Steps of the Sale

Purpose of Each Step	Practice (Salesperson's Role)
Step 1. Greeting	
1. Allows the seller to introduce self to the buyer.	1. Smile and offer the prospect a positive greeting.
2. Allows the prospect to introduce self to the seller.	2. Offer a firm handshake (if culture permits).
3. Allows prospect and seller to exchange business cards.	3. Offer a business card and request a card from the buyer.
Step 2. Warm-up	
1. Gives the prospect time to relax and get comfortable.	1. Talk about the prospect's interests or organization.
2. Gives the seller time to adjust to the environment and compose himself or herself.	2. Breathe deeply, think in positive terms, and smile.
3. Both are given the opportunity to begin evaluating each other's personality, values, likes, and dislikes.	3. Use common sense and understanding of people to evaluate the prospect's personality, values, likes, and dislikes.
Step 3. Qualification	
1. Allows the seller to determine if the prospect is a legitimate buyer or merely a shopper.	1. Thoroughly evaluate the situation and the prospect's needs by asking the "Six Ws" (see the *Glossary*).
2. Allows the prospect to observe and listen to the seller and to evaluate the seller as a possible vendor.	2. Perform professionally— asking logical questions, listening, and responding responsibly.
3. Allows seller to search for possible buyer sales resistance (fear or dislike of the seller, the vendor, the company, service, or product).	3. Ask the prospect about his or her knowledge of (or previous experience with) the service, product, or vendor's organization.

Step 4. Presentation	
1. Based upon the previous steps, this one allows the seller to give the prospect enough data to make a buying decision.	1. Make a personalized presentation that appeals to the buyer's needs, desires, behavior, values, and interests.
2. Leads both prospect and seller to the close in a natural, positive, and collaborative way.	2. Use features, advantages, and benefits that appeal to the prospect and lead to an agreement (the close).

Step 5. Close	
1. Allows the buyer and the seller to agree to • Set an appointment. • Place seller on vendor list. • Allow seller to gather data. • Place an order or trial order. • Set buying and selling terms. • Pay monies owed the vendor. • Meet with the decision maker. • Give presentation or demonstration. • Meet with the buying committee.	1. Seek agreement with the prospect by using • A variety of trial closes. • A courteous, positive, and persistent attitude. • Closes that appeal to the prospect's personality. • The best and strongest closes in later closing stages. • The prospect's ideas and phrases to answer his or her questions or objections.

Source: Adapted from *1st Impressions*, by Andoni Lizardy. Pfeiffer & Company, 1992.

When to Close

The closing process can begin anywhere the salesperson feels it is appropriate. All the seller has to do is make a closing statement or ask a closing question. Yet, the successful implementation of the close is dependent on a variety of factors, such as positioning (implementing the closing process in the right place), timing, commitment, or closing on a buying signal (any indication that the prospect is ready to make a purchase).

I like to offer my prospects a number of closing opportunities during the qualification stage (the third step) of the sale. I often close without making a presentation and have done so effectively and consistently all of my selling career. There is no reason why a seller should not attempt to close a customer before the customer knows all the details of the transaction. There are few rules that govern closing. Some of the best and most ethical salespeople I have ever known close their accounts under the most unusual of circumstances. The first piece of advice I give novice sellers is, simply, *Close*. Ask a closing question or make a closing statement and be ready with a relevant question or response should the prospect reject that close. When is the best time to close? Here is my reply:

> Close early, close late if you must, but always, always, always close on a buying signal.

A seller's chances of closing successfully increase

- Through the wise and professional implementation of trial closes.
- Through the use of closing statements and questions that follow a thorough qualification process (see Table 1-1).
- When the vendor is communicating with a prospect who is fair, willing to listen to the seller, and has an interest in what the salesperson is representing.

Step Five. The Close		
Step of the Sale	Seller's Objective	*Element of the Sale
Close ⟶	Confirms buyer's readiness for ⟶	Action

*See "AIDA" and "Anatomy of the Sale" in the *Glossary*.

Every experienced and professional salesperson and sales manager is aware of the importance of the *close*. The close confirms the buyer's readiness to take action. Traditionally speaking, it is thought of as the final step of the selling process. The close acts as a report card—did the salesperson achieve his or her objectives? It is also the step that many salespeople dread because they fear closing, do not understand the closing process, or do not know how to close effectively or consistently.

Definition of a Close and Closing

Let's take a look at the difference between a *close* and *closing*. A close is any statement of agreement between a buyer and a seller. Closing is the practice of bringing a conclusion to an activity or discussion. Closing is also the act of concluding a sale.

The Purpose and Objectives of a Close

The closing stage is that step when the salesperson

- Requests the prospect's opinion.
- Calls for an answer from the prospect.
- Seeks an agreement with the prospect.

The purpose of the final step of the sale is for both buyer and seller to satisfy their needs and objectives. It is a natural outcome of the previous four steps (greeting, warm-up, qualification, presentation) of the sale. Closing becomes much easier when the first four steps are well executed.

The objective of the close is to bring a conclusion to some aspect of the sale. The salesperson may close on any of the following objectives:

- Setting a future appointment.
- Closing purchase of a product or service.
- Collecting payment of monies owed the vendor.
- Gathering data vital to the sale.
- Making a presentation or demonstration.
- Selling and buying terms
    Size
    Price
    Color
    Flavor
    Quality
    Quantity
    Delivery date
    Financing option
- Meeting with the decision maker, purchasing committee, or other interested parties.
- Receiving consideration as a vendor or as an alternate vendor (placement on the approved vendor's list).
- Obtaining an agreement dealing with some other service- or product-related issue.
- Extending the salesperson special privileges other than those mentioned thus far.

Closing can be approached in a step-by-step way, as outlined in Table 1-2.

Table 1-2 The Steps of a Close
1. Develop a closing objective (complete three or four closing statements or questions). Be prepared with several backup objectives (with appropriate closes) should the prospect reject the initial closing attempts.
2. Listen, identify, and design the close in response to the prospect's
• Fears.
• Values.
• Concerns.
• Personal needs.
• Professional needs.
• Behavior tendencies.
3. Respond to the prospect's buying signals.
4. Know how to trial close and do so regularly using a variety of closes.
5. Learn how to handle rejection and be prepared to react to it in a nondefensive and professional way.
6. Be positive, courageous, and committed to closing.

In other words, the successful closer must want to *help the customer* and must want to *close!* Furthermore, the seller must be *totally prepared* to do so, without the assistance of others. A positive mental attitude is a closer's best friend. Therefore, before meeting with prospects, salespeople should remind themselves, "Our agreement has already been made. I'm here to work out the details."

Closers are most effective in situations where they

- Are comfortable with their prospects.
- Enlist their prospects' active participation in the selling process.
- Can easily demonstrate the service's or product's benefits to their prospects.

Prospects will be cooperative and open to buying others' ideas when they feel comfortable. This comfort level increases with salespeople who

- Smile.
- Listen attentively.
- Are genuinely sincere.
- Display a positive attitude.
- Show concern for their prospects' challenges and needs.
- Discuss features and benefits that are of interest to their listeners.
- Feed back body language and phrases their prospects like and use.
- Behave and speak in ways that their prospects can relate to and appreciate.

When to Initiate the Close

A closing statement or question can be made during any stage of the sale. It is presented here as a distinct step of the sale in order to highlight this critical skill. The successful close depends on three vital success factors:

Positioning
Timing
Commitment

Each of these three words can be applied to the closing process in the following way:

1. *Positioning* for the close is the way salespeople
    - Present their ideas to enhance whatever they are selling; for instance, pointing out to prospects

how features become customer advantages and benefits.

- Predetermine how they will close their prospects. For instance, weaker closes should be used early in the selling process to uncover outstanding issues or questions the prospect might have. In this way, salespeople save their most effective closes for the last stage of the sale.

- Arrange their props (selling aids such as brochures, flip charts, photographs, and samples) to sell their ideas, products, and services. For instance, these individuals may show their prospects samples or brochures about how their products are produced, or they may show them letters from satisfied customers.

2. *Timing* the close refers to the moment salespeople

- Decide to initiate their closing attempts.
- Present their ideas, features, advantages, and benefits.
- Introduce their props (brochures, flip charts, photographs, and samples).

3. *Commitment* refers to the dedication closers bring to the closing process. For example:

- Do they sound and look professional?
- Do they sincerely appear to want their prospects' business?
- Do they appear committed to what they are saying and doing?
- Do they appear to be enthusiastic and sincere about what they are offering?

There are successful salespeople who sell well despite their lack of timing and positioning. But their lack of tact regarding these two disciplines makes their job that much more difficult. Yet they are effective because their level of enthusiasm, sincerity, and desire to succeed overshadow all else. Perhaps this best demonstrates the importance of commitment and enthusiasm as they relate to selling.

Table 1-3 demonstrates when a trial close or close most commonly appears in the five steps of the sale.

Table 1-3 The Anatomy of the Sale When to Close or Trial Close	
Legend: Step where the close or trial close is most commonly used ✓	
Step of the Sale	Where Trial Close or Close is Employed
1. Greeting	1.
2. Warm-up	2.
3. Qualification	3. ✓
4. Presentation	4. ✓
5. Closing	5. ✓

Chapter Summary

1. The close is the fifth step of the selling process.
   - Step 1. Greeting
   - Step 2. Warm-up
   - Step 3. Qualification
   - Step 4. Presentation
   - Step 5. Close

2. A close is any statement of agreement between the buyer and seller. Closing is the practice of bringing a conclusion to an activity or discussion. Closing is also the act of concluding a sale.

3. The objective of the close is to bring a conclusion to some aspect of the sale. You may close your prospect for

- A future appointment.
- Actual purchase of a product or service.
- Payment of monies owed the vendor.
- Allowing the seller to gather data vital to the sale.
- Allowing the seller to make a presentation or demonstration.
- Meeting with the decision maker, purchasing committee, or other interested parties.
- Consideration as a vendor or as an alternate vendor (placement on the approved vendor's list).
- Selling and buying terms
  Size
  Price
  Color
  Flavor
  Quality
  Quantity
  Delivery date
  Financing option
- Agreement dealing with some other service- or product-related issue.

- Extending the salesperson special privileges other than those mentioned thus far.

4. The steps of a close are

   - Develop a closing objective (complete three or four closing statements or questions). Be prepared with several backup objectives (with appropriate closes) should the prospect reject the initial closing attempts.

   - Listen, identify, and design the close in response to the prospect's

     Fears

     Values

     Concerns

     Personal needs

     Professional needs

     Behavior tendencies

   - Respond to the prospect's buying signals.

   - Know how to trial close and do so regularly using a variety of closes.

   - Learn how to handle rejection well and be prepared to react to it in a nondefensive and professional way.

   - Be positive, courageous, and committed to closing.

5. You can help the prospect feel comfortable and increase the likelihood of a sale by

   - Smiling.

   - Expressing sincerity.

   - Listening attentively.

   - Displaying a positive attitude.

   - Showing concern for the prospect's challenges and needs.

- Discussing features and benefits that are of interest to the prospect.
- Feeding back body language and phrases the prospect likes and uses.
- Behaving and speaking in ways that the prospect can relate to and appreciate.

6. Your closing successes are dependent on three vital factors:
   - Positioning
   - Timing
   - Commitment

7. You do not have to wait until the end of the sale to close. You can trial close during the qualification and presentation steps of the sale.

2

Types of Closes

Closing well is only a small part of the selling process. Success-fully concluding a transaction is a byproduct of professional and positive seller-prospect communications.

"I want you to teach my salespeople how to close," the president of one of our client's companies commanded.

"Fine," I answered. "Why did you select the close as the first topic?"

"Because we need to make money now. The more you close, the more money you make. It's that simple," he replied crisply.

"Have you ever given your people sales training?" I asked.

"Three years ago," he answered.

"Did you cover the closing process with them?"

"Yes."

"Were they receptive to the instruction?"

"Our better sellers were, but the balance of the staff wasn't."

"Did you reinforce the training within ninety days of offering it the first time?"

"No. We normally give them a training program once a year. We just haven't had the money or the time to train them the last two years."

"Few salespeople excel with intermittent training. The space between annual programs is far too long. You're wasting your training money trying to train your people once a year."

"It sure shows now," he remarked in a low tone.

"How good are your salespeople at qualifying a prospect or customer?"

"What do you mean by qualifying?"

"Determining what a customer wants."

"You mean questions the seller asks to determine the buyer's needs?"

"Correct."

"I really can't comment on that. I guess that's not a good statement for a CEO to make, is it?"

"At least it's an honest response. Are your salespeople effective?"

"They're well-experienced," he answered softly, paused, and then continued, "I didn't answer your question, did I?"

"I think you did. Let me take a guess at their situation: your salespeople are well-experienced but not as effective as you would like them to be."

"Right. They're capable of much higher production."

"Why are they failing to close an acceptable number of sales?"

"They don't know how to close, and often they're not asking our prospects the right questions."

"You mean they're not qualifying your customers and prospects thoroughly."

"Yes, they're not qualifying as thoroughly as they should be. All right," he said with a chuckle, "let's start them with a course in qualifying. Better yet, let's start them with a course covering all the basics of selling. And remember—they're good salespeople; we just want to make them better."

His sales force was similar to the many other sales training organizations we meet. They were well-tenured in sales and understood their products and services. Unfortunately, they were not as sensitive to their customers' needs as they should have been. This lack of sensitivity led to a loss of many sales.

Evaluating Your Closing Style
Part I—Attitude

Each of the following chapters includes a self-assessment exercise for those interested in evaluating their closing style. These exercises were developed during a fifteen-year period with over 10,000 salespeople, sales managers, and other customer contact people in nearly 2,500 actual selling and customer contact situations and over 8,200 roleplaying exercises evaluated by myself and the Lizardy Associates assessment team.

The questions, answers, scoring values, and classifications are based on the performances and attitudes displayed by the many people my associates and I worked with, trained, and critiqued during the previously mentioned period.

Exercise Suggestions

In the interest of accuracy, please review the following suggestions:

- Move as rapidly as possible through the exercise, avoiding overanalyzing any question or answer.

- If you encounter difficulty in responding to any of the following questions objectively, ask someone who is experienced and qualified in sales (and who has watched you sell in a variety of situations) to respond to these questions as if he or she were you.

- Avoid guessing or using the process of deduction to arrive at any answer you do not know. Select only those answers that indicate the way you actually perform—not the way you think you should sell or would like to sell. In other words, avoid responding to a statement if your normal practice differs from it.

This exercise and the others found in this book are neither tests nor contests. These studies and the Probable Tendencies tables that follow them allow review of your performance and awareness of the closing process. Each one deals with a specific aspect of closing.

Part I. Attitude
Part II. Implementation
Part III. Closing phrases you may tend to use
Part IV. Closing classifications you most rely on

These reviews are relativity exercises that allow you to select your most common practice from several options. Because of the scoring process, try to limit your selections to one choice in every section. If you feel that two answers apply to you, you may check both selections and then halve their numerical value when scoring the exercise. Each statement and choice realistically reflect actual closing situations and options. All of this should help you to understand that your conduct and attitude affect the way you communicate, sell, and close.

Each study provides the opportunity to evaluate which of three closing styles you are most likely to exhibit in relationship to the exercise's topic. Regardless of how well you do, the most important score is reflected in your performance, your sense of self-worth, and your customers' willingness to reward your behavior with their patronage.

Exercise
Closing Styles Study
Part I—Attitude

Instructions

Check the letter next to the answer that is most accurate. You may check a second option if a second answer also applies. For example:

0. I like to close
   - a. Rapidly
   - ✓ b. In a subtle way
   - ✓✓ c. After I get to know the prospect

In making your choices

- Do not mark any phrase you are uncertain of or that does not apply.
- Check the *Glossary* or *Index* for any word that is unfamiliar.
- Be as honest as possible and mark the way you actually perform or behave.

---

1. I feel that the purpose of the close is to
   - a. Get a commitment to buy from the prospect.
   - ✓ b. Bring a conclusion to some aspect of the sale.
   - c. Please the customer.

2. This statement best describes me:
   - a. I enjoy difficult prospects and difficult closing situations.
   - ✓ b. I dislike closing when prospects offer hard objections.
   - c. I am premeditated yet flexible in closing.

3. Of the following, the one that comes closest to my closing weakness is

   a. I close too often and too assertively.

   ✓ b. I don't close as often and assertively as I should.

   c. I sometimes wait too long to close.

4. I consider the most important step of the sale to be the

   ✓ a. Qualification.

   b. Presentation.

   c. Close.

5. I feel that a prospect's objection is an indication that

   a. The prospect is still interested in my product or service.

   b. I should close harder.

   ✓ c. I am not doing as well as I would like to be doing.

6. If the prospect rejects three of my closes within five minutes

   ✓ a. I recognize that this person probably isn't going to make a purchase.

   b. I become more determined in my closing attempts.

   c. I deal with each objection as it warrants and then trial close again.

7. I see the closing process as something that occurs

   a. Whenever the customer initiates the close.

   ✓ b. Throughout the entire selling process.

   c. Whenever the seller initiates it.

8. When a prospect strongly objects to my closing attempts, I
   a. Answer promptly with a direct response.
   b. Avoid dealing directly with the prospect's objections.
   c. Help the prospect answer the objection and then close again.

9. If a buyer is extremely rude when objecting to my closes, I
   a. Usually take the objections personally.
   b. Try to uncover the cause and diffuse the buyer's hostility.
   c. Meet the buyer's hostility head on (assertively or aggressively).

10. I feel that closing the sale
   a. Is controlled by the seller.
   b. Is something that cannot be controlled.
   c. Is a natural byproduct of the communication between buyer and seller.

Scoring
Closing Styles Study
Part I—Attitude

Legend

PO — Pressure-Oriented or Aggressive Closer
CA — Closure-Aversive or Noncloser
PS — Professional or Subtle Closer

Instructions

From the previous *Exercise,* circle the same letters below, including the score.

After completing this section, proceed to the *Score Box*. Make certain your answers reflect the way you actually interact with your prospects and customers.

1. I feel that the purpose of the close is to
   a. PO
   b. PS
   c. CA

2. This statement best describes me:
   a. PO
   b. CA
   c. PS

3. Of the following, the one that comes closest to my closing weakness is
   a. PO
   b. CA
   c. PS

4. I consider the most important step of the sale to be the
   a. PS
   b. CA
   c. PO

5. I feel that a prospect's objection is an indication that
   a. PS
   b. PO
   c. CA

6. If the prospect rejects three of my closes within five minutes:
   a. CA
   b. PO
   c. PS

7. I see the closing process as something that occurs
   a. CA
   b. PS
   c. PO

8. When a prospect strongly objects to my closing attempts, I
   a. PO
   b. CA
   c. PS

9. If a buyer is extremely rude in objecting to my closes, I
   a. CA
   b. PS
   c. PO

10. I feel that closing the sale
    a. PO
    b. CA
    c. PS

Score Box
Closing Styles Study
Part I—Attitude

Instructions

Each of your checked answers is worth ten points. Halve the value (five points each) wherever you have selected two answers under the same question. Total your score for each category and place it on the line to the right of the appropriate classification.

PS 30
CA 45
PO 25

Closing Tendency	Total Points
PO — Pressure-Oriented Closer	_25_
CA — Closure-Aversive Closer	_45_
PS — Professional Closer	_30_

Find your scores for each category (PO, CA, PS) on Table 2-1. If your total score for any category is 70 or 40, read both phrases (just above and below that score). The analysis is based solely on the accuracy of your selections. It reviews only the technical aspects of your closing practices.

Table 2-1 Probable Tendencies
Closing Styles Study
Part I—Attitude

PO Pressure-Oriented	CA Closure-Aversive	PS Professional
70 – 100 Points		
You possess an aggressive attitude toward closing. You may feel people who are unassertive are weak and waste your time.	You possess a passive attitude toward closing. You dislike overly aggressive closers. You avoid closes that are pressure-oriented.	You possess a positive attitude toward closing. Correctly, you feel that you have the right to ask others for their business.
40 – 70 Points		
You are an assertive and direct closer. Your open attitude and willingness to close allow you to succeed where others stumble or fail.	You are inconsistent in the way you close. Your closes may vary from tactful to assertive, depending on the people involved.	You have a positive and healthy closing attitude. You close well, but need more practice to obtain the superior results you are capable of.
0 – 40 Points		
You are tactful in the way that you close and you appreciate those who treat you likewise.	You have no difficulty being assertive in your selling efforts and are not afraid to close.	Your closing success is greatly affected by your mood, which can be a major liability.

If your responses are correct and your awareness is a reflection of your attitude toward closing, the assessment will be accurate. Other critical factors that impact your attitude (for example, appearance, body language, confidence, voice, product or service knowledge, and the sub-elements of the sale) are not factored into this study.

For a more personal and in-depth review, see the section at the back of this book titled *The Lizardy Associates Closing Styles (Complimentary) Analysis.* Regardless of how you scored, review the practices recommended in this book. Look for those techniques that can help you, and put them to work as soon as possible.

More About Your Score

The top score reveals your primary or basic closing style (note what aspect of closing is addressed in each exercise). Your second highest score is normally considered your backup style. The backup style is the way you relate to yourself and to others if you have lost confidence in your basic style. Few people display one style exclusively. Therefore, you will most likely display a mixture of behaviors from your two categories.

If you scored 70–100 points in any one category, you may

- Display the behaviors of that category almost exclusively in your business dealings.
- Be convinced that your primary style is the only way you can deal with others successfully.
- Experience difficulties dealing with customers who are not comfortable with your primary way of relating to others.

If you scored 50–69 points in any one category, you display the behaviors of that category most of the time in your business dealings.

If you scored fewer than 50 points in the Professional category, consider doing the following:

- Improving your sensitivity and responsiveness toward your customers.
- Practicing the skills involved in achieving the objectives of a close by videotaping simulated sales and customer contact situations and allowing a qualified person to critique you during the playback of those tapes.
- Seeking coaching and counseling or training and development assistance in the following areas: listening, basic communications, basic sales, customer relations skills, psychology of selling, video roleplaying as both vendor and customer, self-esteem building, time management, customer sensitivity training, stress management, and closing terminology.

Note: Contradictions in the *Attitude* section of the *Closing Styles Study* may indicate some conflicts in your closing style.

Three Types of Salespeople

Professional purchasing agents, as well as individual consumers, have often commented or complained that most salespeople seem to exhibit several types of behavior. These buyers use expressions such as helpful, indifferent, knowledgeable, ignorant, concerned, aloof, self-centered, and pressure-oriented to describe the various types of vendor representatives.

Salespeople can be grouped into three categories: *professional*, *pressure-oriented*, and *closure-aversive*. These categories are also referred to as selling tendencies and communication tendencies. Following is a brief description of each.

Professional Salesperson

The professional salesperson is a problem solver and a competent self-manager who is most concerned with

- Satisfying the customer's needs.
- Dealing in an ethical and professional manner.
- Establishing a positive and professional image.
- Maintaining high standards regarding productivity, profitability, and performance.
- Attracting long-term business relationships that yield repeat profitable business, productive relationships, and positive references.

This type of person is difficult to find since there are so many practices the professional is expected to execute well. For example, this individual must

- Be an effective listener.
- Be a persuasive communicator.
- Be an effective mediator between the vendor's organization and the customer.
- So value the customer's interests that personal short-term needs or gains are set aside if they threaten the relationship with the customer.
- Be a subtle closer. (This most definitely includes customer-contact people, who sometimes overlook the importance of their customer-related communication and selling skills.)

The professional salesperson is consistent, fair, honest, and competent. This person is usually viewed by customers as someone who is responsible, caring, loyal, and consultative. The professional vendor believes, "My success is due to my high standards and ethical behavior with both my employer and customer. Let's do what is best for all concerned."

Strength-wise, the professional person is

- A self-starter.
- Able to satisfy both task and human demands.
- Willing to sacrifice immediate gains for long-term results.

As for weaknesses, the professional person

- May not work well with inept superiors.
- May not like customers who are untrustworthy.
- May not like an employer who is not customer sensitive.
- May not immediately produce the kinds of results an employer desires.

Pressure-Oriented Salesperson

The pressure-oriented salesperson (also known as a one-time salesperson) is most concerned with taking care of his or her immediate objectives. This seller has little interest in the customer's needs. The pressure-oriented salesperson's greatest concern is with short-term personal results and gains. The phrase "one time" implies that this person is so self-centered or brusque that most customers will do business with this vendor only once (if these customers have the option to buy from other vendors).

The pressure-oriented salesperson rarely attracts repeat business, because many customers and prospects view this individual as abrasive, uncaring, and unworthy of their patronage. This type of person is overly concerned with the task at hand and displays little sensitivity to the customer's personality needs (for example, emotions, ego, fears, and sensitivities). The one-time vendor fears wasting time or losing any opportunity to gain more business. The pressure-oriented salesperson views tension and pressure as natural communication tools, not realizing that many customers may think of these techniques as negative practices. Customers rarely view pressure-oriented salespeople as loyal to their employers or to their clients. The pressure-oriented person believes in the motto "Do what it takes to make the sale."

Strength-wise, the pressure-oriented salesperson

- Is a self-starter.
- Is willing to tackle difficult assignments.
- Will not accept the word *no* as an answer.

As for weaknesses, the pressure-oriented person

- Can be insensitive and impolite.
- May not know when to compromise.
- May not deal well with routine work.
- Does not like *nonrevenue-producing duties* such as after-sales support activities.

Closure-Aversive Salesperson

The closure-aversive salesperson (sometimes referred to as customer-aversive) is usually a passive individual who desires to avoid conflict at almost any cost. The closure-aversive type is more interested in maintaining a peaceful environment and the superficial trappings of a positive relationship than in achieving results.

The closure-aversive salesperson does not like to close or undertake any role that may create tension or cause discomfort. While closure-aversive and pressure-oriented salespeople are nearly opposite in their behavior, they do have one thing in common—they are both self-centered because they are absorbed with their own feelings, needs, and emotions.

This self-centeredness, however, is expressed differently. In the case of the closure-aversive individual, that self-concern manifests itself in self-protection against rejection and any affront to the seller's sensitivities. This individual is more than willing to pass up developing more business if it means that there might be a difficult moment between the vendor and the customer. Most of the closure-aversive salesperson's customers will view this individual as loyal to his or her employer. The closure-aversive person believes in the phrase "Peace at any price."

Strengthwise, the closure-aversive salesperson is

- Sensitive.
- A team player.
- Good at routine work with positive clients in familiar settings.

As for weaknesses, the closure-aversive salesperson

- Is not a self-starter.
- May not deal well with confrontations.
- Accepts *no* as an answer too frequently and too quickly.

Regardless of our biases or preferences, all three types of salespeople have an important role to play. This book can help you determine which behavior you most often display in your closing efforts and what you can do to improve your closing results.

The Best Type of Closer

There is no such thing as the best type of closer. There are only different types of closers. Each type can be successful, depending on a variety of factors:

- The relationship between the prospect and the salesperson.
- The prospect's personal and professional needs and constraints.
- The salesperson's personal and professional needs and constraints.
- The salesperson's behavior, values, emotional makeup, and applied intelligence.
- The salesperson's positioning, timing, and commitment to each of the involved parties.

If you are getting the desired results through your closing efforts and are happy with those results, then your closing style is the right one for you. It is hoped that the previous exercise has helped identify some of your closing strengths and needs.

Types of Closes

To become a successful closer, a salesperson needs to know what types of closes there are and when to apply each type. The many ways to close can be classified as

1. Low-risk (also known as positive closes)
2. High-risk (also known as hostile closes)

Closes can also be classified as

1. Direct closes
2. Indirect closes

Salespeople should use positive closes whenever possible. *Positive* or *low-risk closes* are those closing statements or questions that encourage positive and collaborative relations between buyers and sellers. The customer tends to feel comfortable and unafraid of the salesperson who uses positive or low-risk closes. Whenever possible, the selling agent should avoid overly aggressive, threatening, or otherwise hostile closing statements.

High-risk or *hostile closes* are precarious closing statements and questions that pressure a prospect into making a buying decision. Such closes must be used judiciously. Using high-risk closes only when all other efforts have failed is a wise policy for sellers to follow.

Closes may also be direct or indirect. A *direct close* is a question or statement that calls for the prospect to make an immediate buying decision. An *indirect close* is an unapparent closing technique that encourages an agreement between buyer and seller.

Most indirect closes are considered to be low risk because they are designed to make the prospect feel comfortable with the selling and buying process.

Most direct closes are considered to be high risk because they create stressful circumstances for the buyer. The seller, for instance, may apply pressure on the prospect by

1. Demanding an immediate decision.
2. Issuing an ultimatum, such as
   - Threatening to withdraw an offer if the prospect alters any of the terms of sale.

- Threatening to offer some exclusive advantage to the prospect's competitor if that prospect refuses to buy.

3. Threatening the customer with some other type of loss, such as loss of availability, price increase, or delayed delivery time.

High-Risk Closes

A high-risk close may cause the buyer to react in some unexpected way. It also may cause the prospect to feel defensive, inferior, or otherwise uncomfortable. Here are some examples:

- "Do you want to buy one?"
- "You should buy this item—everyone else has."
- "This is a smart move—buy it."
- "The price is going up tomorrow. Better buy now!"
- "It's our last one. If you want it, you'd better decide now!"
- "If I could show you a way of saving money using this product, would you buy it?"

Note: This is a high-risk close because use of the word buy calls for the prospect to make a decision and to spend money now.

High-risk closes have their purpose in sales. A salesperson may use a high-risk close when

1. The prospect's personality responds better to a high- versus a low-risk close. Aggressive prospects tend to respond more positively to high-risk closes than do customers who are highly sensitive and security-conscious.

2. All other types of closes have failed and the seller has nothing to lose.

A salesperson should avoid using high-risk closes with customers who are easily intimidated.

Low-Risk Closes

Low-risk closes are those closing statements that minimize the odds of the prospect feeling uncomfortable with the salesperson's attempt to close. A low-risk close does not necessarily increase the chances for a successful close—it only minimizes the chances of a negative or unexpected response. For example:

- "You would like one if it satisfied all your needs, wouldn't you?"
- "Would you prefer a green or red one?"

Note: This is an example of an indirect close, as the seller asks what the buyer *prefers*, not which item the customer wants to buy.

- "If I could show you a way of saving money using our services, would you be interested in listening to how it could put dollars into your pocket?"

Note: This is a low-risk close because the seller asks the buyer if he or she would "be interested in listening..." Listening does not cost the prospect anything more than a small amount of time.

Table 2-2 separates closes into high-risk and low-risk types.

Table 2-2 Types of Closes High-Risk vs. Low-Risk Closes	
High-Risk Closes	**Low-Risk Closes**
Pity	Self
Guilt	Choice
Assumptive	Add-on
Intimidation	Preference
Reverse Psychology	Trial Offer
Asking for the Order	Trial Order
Misstated Higher Quantity	Five Yeses
	Minor Point
	Loaded Yes
	Financial Balance Sheet
	Weighing or Ben Franklin
	Backup or Alternate Vendor
Closes That Can Be Classified as Either High-Risk or Low-Risk Depending on How They Are Used Higher Reference Conditional or Barter Third-Party Reference	

Which type of close would best serve the selling situation depends greatly on the client's personality, the salesperson's selling style, each party's needs, time constraints, and the risk factors involved.

Direct Closes

A direct close is one in which the seller attempts to close the prospect with a bold statement or question. Since direct closes are strong closing questions or statements, most are also considered to be high-risk closes. For example: "You do want to buy this today, don't you?"

Indirect Closes

An indirect close is a nonaggressive question or statement that tests the prospect's readiness to make a buying decision. An indirect close is one that

1. Does not intimidate the prospect.
2. May call for an opinion or feeling rather than a commitment.
3. Helps the seller evaluate the prospect's present position. Indirect closing guidelines are similar to those that apply to low-risk closes. For example: "Will you be using this at home or at the office?"

Table 2-3 separates closes into direct and indirect types.

Table 2-3 Types of Closes Direct vs. Indirect Closes	
Direct Closes	**Indirect Closes**
Pity	Self
Add-on	Choice
Trial Offer	Preference
Trial Order	Minor Point
Five Yeses	Reverse Psychology
Puppy Dog	Financial Balance Sheet
Assumptive	Weighing or Ben Franklin
Loaded Yes	
Asking for the Order	

Closes That Can Be Classified as Direct or Indirect, Depending Upon How They Are Used

Guilt
Intimidation
Higher Reference
Conditional or Barter
Third-Party Reference
Misstated Higher Quantity
Backup or Alternate Vendor

Trial Closes

A trial close (also known as a throw-away close) is a subtle question or statement that tests a prospect's readiness to buy. For example, a binder salesperson might say to a customer, "Do you prefer a high-quality finish on your binders or something less expensive?"

Trial closes prepare both the customer and seller for the actual close. Using a variety of trial closes to influence the customer's decision is an excellent way to position one's strongest closing statement. Customers are often ready to buy before the sellers are even aware of it. That is another reason why trial closes should be employed early—to determine the level of buyer readiness to purchase.

Any close can be employed as a trial close, but some are easier to use in this capacity than others. Table 2-4 offers conventional closes that can help a seller ascertain a prospect's willingness to proceed with a purchase.

Table 2-4 Types of Closes Trial Closes
Guilt Close
Choice Close
Trial-Offer Close
Preference Close
Trial-Order Close
Puppy Dog Close
Minor Point Close
Intimidation Close
Assumptive Close
Loaded Yes Close
Reverse Psychology Close
Conditional or Barter Close
Financial Balance Sheet Close
Weighing or Ben Franklin Close
Backup or Alternate Vendor Close

Trial Close Guidelines

Most trial closes tend to be indirect closes, so trial closing guidelines are similar to those that apply to indirect closes. Trial closes should

- Call for a simple response from the prospect.
- Call for a low-risk commitment from the buyer.
- Encourage a positive response from the listener.
- Help the salesperson to determine the prospect's buying readiness.
- Provide the salesperson with an opportunity for other discussions if the trial close fails. Here are some examples of trial closes:
  1. "Were you thinking of purchasing this robe for yourself or for a friend?"
  2. "Do you feel your boss would prefer taking care of this matter by check or charge?"

The salesperson should keep the closing process positive. To do so, the seller must be conditioned not to respond emotionally or negatively to the word *no* or to other forms of rejection.

Chapter Summary

1. Salespeople can be grouped into three categories:
   - Professional
   - Pressure-oriented
   - Closure-aversive
2. Closes can be classified as low-risk (positive) closes or high-risk (hostile) closes.

3. **Low-risk** or **positive closes** are those that create positive and collaborative relations between you and your buyers.

4. **High-risk,** sometimes known as **hostile** or **negative closes,** are closing ploys that create tension for the prospect.

5. Closes can also be classified as direct closes or indirect closes.

6. A **direct close** is a question or statement that you may use to encourage a prospect to make an immediate decision regarding the purchase. Direct closes tend to be high risk.

7. An **indirect close** is an unapparent closing technique that encourages an agreement between buyer and seller.

8. A **trial close** (also known as a **throw-away close**) is a subtle question or statement that tests a prospect's readiness to buy.

9. Trial closes should
   - Call for a simple response from the prospect.
   - Call for a low-risk commitment from the buyer.
   - Encourage a positive response from the listener.
   - Help the salesperson to determine the prospect's buying readiness.
   - Provide the salesperson with an opportunity for other discussions if the trial close fails.

3

THE LOW-RISK CLOSES

Definitions and Models

Successful salespeople are individuals who have mastered the art of selecting the selling style and close that appeals most to their customers.

The stranger next to me was obviously trying to get my attention, but I stared away from him, choosing to watch the traffic instead of talking with him. My companion also noticed the man, but she too looked away.

He's probably trying to sell something, I thought. The streets of Cairo, Egypt are filled with beggars, sellers, and tourists.

"You are from the United States?" he finally said, trying to break the silence between the three of us.

"Yes," I answered.

His whole manner brightened as he turned to face us squarely, "Well, welcome to Cairo."

"Thank you."

"Your first time in Cairo?"

"No."

"Good. Then you must like our city to return. Thank you, it is kind of you to return. Have you seen much of the city on this trip?"

"No."

"That is unfortunate. You must take the time to see the Pyramids and the museums."

"Good idea."

"You are here on business?"

"Yes."

"Very good. I am in business, too."

My companion and I were now eagerly awaiting the changing of the traffic light so we could cross the intersection and get away from our unwanted acquaintance.

"What part of the U.S. are you from?" the inquisitive man insisted on knowing.

"The West," I answered hurriedly as we began crossing the intersection.

"Oh, very nice." His Egyptian accent became much more apparent. "I lived there too for a while in Ventura, California. Nice place."

"Yes, nice place," I replied.

"What business are you in?" he asked as we neared the opposite curb.

"Sales. We train salespeople and their managers."

"Ah, so you own your business?"

"Yes."

"So do I. A very good business not far from here."

"That's nice," I commented as we neared the shop we wanted to visit. "Well, have a good day."

"Oh, thank you. I have a perfume business," he continued politely as if we had not completed our conversation. "You must visit my shop and see my business."

This guy is trying to close us on going to his shop. How bold.

"Sorry," I added rapidly, "this is where we part. Nice talking with you."

"Oh, yes," he stated with a smile. "It is very close."

He's still trying to close us.

I made a mistake and asked, "What?"

"My shop. It is very close. Come see our perfumes. The lady here, I am sure, would like to see how we make perfume from the petals of exotic flowers. We gather these flowers from India, China, and from Egypt, too."

"Thank you, but no," I replied. "We have no time."

I knew I was making a mistake by talking with the man, but his manner was so kind and endearing that I did not want to walk away from him abruptly.

"Perhaps some other time," I added with a smile.

"And you, lady? Would you like to see my shop? It has been in my family for many generations. We have the finest perfumes. You are not obligated to buy anything. Come, it is very close," he kept insisting in a persistent yet gentle manner.

This is a mistake, I thought. *Oh, what the heck. This guy is so persistent and yet polite, he deserves a chance. And who knows—maybe I'll get a story out of this.*

I looked at my friend and she just smiled.

Well, I guess it's my decision, I thought.

"How close is it?" I asked.

"Very close, sir. Just around the corner," he answered eagerly as he led the way.

Just around the corner, I bet. Probably right down a dark alley, I mumbled to myself.

Three blocks later and half-winded, I demanded, "Just where is this corner?"

"Right here," he said with a chuckle as he led us down a wide side street.

Well, at least it's not a dark alley.

"Hey!" I shouted as I stopped. "This is enough."

"Yes, sir," he replied from across the street as he opened the door of a shop. "We are here already. See, it was a very short walk. Very pleasant. Yes, very nice. Do come in. I am so proud of my shop. You will like it. You will see."

My companion started laughing and said, "He's pretty bright, isn't he?"

"Bright enough to get a couple of Americans to follow him through Cairo."

"Why are we doing this?" she asked.

"I don't know. I guess because he's so insistent."

"This is crazy."

"You're telling me."

"Come, come," he said as he held the door open in welcome.

We both smiled at our guide as we entered the shop. I was struck immediately by a strange mixture of perfumes. At one moment the room was filled with a light floral smell, while the next moment the scents were heavy, sweet, and overpowering.

"This is my associate, Mohammed. He runs the shop," our guide stated as he motioned us to sit down.

"Please sit down," Mohammed suggested firmly with a smile.

These two have their selling act down to a science. The first one grabs the prospect off the street, and this one must be the closer. What a routine.

The next few minutes were filled with Middle Eastern pleasantries, perfume presentations, and subtle closes. Mohammed was as professional as his associate, and both were skilled in the art of the soft or low-risk close. Their selling styles were similar, in that they showed their prospects great respect and kindness, and an extremely accommodating and polite manner. Yet they never stopped closing. Subtle close after subtle close led us right to where they wanted us.

For those of you who are wondering, no, we did not buy any perfume, although their routine was very persuasive. But as predicted, I did get a good story.

Evaluating Your Closing Style
Part II—Implementation

Before you read further, you might want to participate in the following closing style exercise dealing with how you implement the closing process. If you have not read the instructions that precede the self-assessment exercise in

Chapter 2, you might review those sections at this time (*Evaluating Your Closing Style, Part I—Attitude* and *Exercise Suggestions*).

Exercise
Closing Styles Study
Part II—Implementation

Instructions

Check the letter next to the answer that is most accurate. You may check a second option if a second answer also applies. For example:

0. I like to close

    a. Rapidly

✓ b. In a subtle way

✓✓ c. After I get to know the prospect

In making your choices

- Do not mark any phrase you are uncertain of or that does not apply.
- Check the *Glossary* or *Index* for any word that is unfamiliar.
- Be as honest as possible and mark the way you actually perform or behave.

A continuation of the Closing Styles Study Exercise, this section begins with number 11.

11. With difficult prospects, I attempt to close
    a. Once or twice per call, at most.
    √b. Whenever the closing opportunities present themselves.
    c. As often and directly as possible, regardless of the prospect's mood.

12. When I hear a buying signal, I
    a. Trial close immediately.
    b. Respond properly and then trial close.
    √c. Would say my performance varies.

13. I use a trial close when I am attempting to
    a. Determine if the prospect likes me or not.
    √b. Evaluate the prospect's feelings or readiness to buy.
    c. I don't believe in trial closes. I give my prospect one chance to buy and that's that.

14. I attempt to trial close
    a. Often, regardless of the prospect's attitude.
    b. Sparingly and as indirectly as possible.
    √c. Often, according to how appropriate a trial close is at that instant.

15. I know that the success of my closing attempts relies on
    a. My qualification and presentation efforts.
    b. How often and how hard I close.
    √c. The customer's attitude toward me.

16. Of these choices, I use this close or a similar one:

    a. Since your boss (or spouse) likes this model, you should buy it.

    b. Is there anything else I can say to help you make a decision?

    √ c. When is the best time for us to start your service, Monday or Tuesday?

17. My prospects would say that I am

    a. Closing oriented.

    √ b. Loyal to my employer.

    √√ c. Problem-solving oriented.

18. I am most likely to close

    a. The first chance I get.

    b. When I hear a buying signal.

    √ c. I don't close—I wait for my prospects to tell me when they are ready.

19. If asked, my prospects would claim that I close

    a. In a very aggressive way.

    √ b. In a very low-key way.

    c. In a premeditated way.

20. I get the action (results) I want from the prospect by

    a. Asking the prospect for the order.

    b. Using a variety of different closes.

    √ c. Using my strongest close as early as possible.

Scoring
Closing Styles Study
Part II—Implementation

Legend

> PO — Pressure-Oriented or Aggressive Closer
> CA — Closure-Aversive or Noncloser
> PS — Professional or Subtle Closer

Instructions

From the previous *Exercise,* circle the same letters below, including the score.

After completing this section, proceed to the *Score Box.* Make certain your answers reflect the way you actually interact with your prospects and customers.

11. With difficult prospects, I attempt to close

  a. CA
  b. PS
  c. PO

12. When I hear a buying signal, I

  a. PO
  b. PS
  c. CA

13. I use a trial close when I am attempting to

  a. CA
  b. PS
  c. PO

14. I attempt to trial close

  a. PO
  b. CA
  c. PS

15. I know that the success of my closing attempts relies on

    a. PS
    b. PO
    c. CA

16. Of these choices, I use this close or a similar one:

    a. PO
    b. CA
    c. PS

17. My prospects would say that I am

    a. PO
    b. CA
    c. PS

18. I am most likely to close

    a. PO
    b. PS
    c. CA

19. If asked, my prospects would claim that I close

    a. PO
    b. CA
    c. PS

20. I get the action (results) I want from the prospect by

    a. CA
    b. PS
    c. PO

Score Box
Closing Styles Study
Part II—Implementation

Instructions

Each of your checked answers is worth ten points. Halve the value (five points each) wherever you have selected two answers under the same question. Total your score for each category and place it on the line to the right of the appropriate classification.

	Closing Tendency	**Total Points**
PO —	Pressure-Oriented Closer	70
CA —	Closure-Aversive Closer	45
PS —	Professional Closer	45

Find your scores for each category (PO, CA, PS) on Table 3-1. If your total score for any category is 70 or 40, read both phrases (just above and below that score). The analysis is based solely on the accuracy of your selections. It reviews only the technical aspects of your closing practices.

If your responses are correct and your awareness is a reflection of your attitude toward closing, the assessment will be accurate. Other critical factors that impact your attitude (for example, appearance, body language, confidence, voice, product or service knowledge, and the sub-elements of the sale) are not factored into this study.

Table 3-1 Probable Tendencies Closing Styles Study Part II—Implementation		
PO Pressure-Oriented	CA Closure-Aversive	PS Professional
70 – 100 Points		
Many people will view you as a fearless and assertive person. You enjoy challenge and the stimulation of the closing process. You can be a powerful and relentless closer.	You desire amiable and positive relations with your customers. You avoid conflict at almost all costs. You are frequently overly cautious in your dealings with prospects and customers.	You can be persuasive, flexible, and effective as a closer. Your success depends greatly on your values, desires, and commitment to selling. You can close well.
40 – 70 Points		
You understand the importance of closing in a timely and efficient way. You can be a "hard" closer.	Sometimes you try too hard to please others. You may be overly sensitive to peer, prospect, and customer criticisms.	Your closing efforts can range from exceptional to average, depending on your aspirations, mood, and training.
0 – 40 Points		
Others may view you as responsbile and prudent in the way you deal with prospects and customers	You are willing to close. You can vary your closes to suit your prospects and closing goals.	Expand your closing repertoire, especially if you are in business-to-business sales.

For a more personal and in-depth review, see the section at the back of this book titled *The Lizardy Associates Closing Styles (Complimentary) Analysis.* Regardless of how you scored, review the practices recommended in this book. Look for those techniques that can help you, and put them to work as soon as possible.

Examining the Close

This book examines the following aspects of each type of close:

1. Defining the close
2. Most effective use of the close
3. When not to use this close
4. Examples of the close
5. If the buyer replies to the close in a positive way
6. If the close is rejected

Where appropriate, real-life closing phrases are offered. You can rephrase and use these statements and questions to apply to future closing situations.

Many Ways to Close

There are, of course, many ways to close. The greater a salesperson's repertoire of closes, the better the chances of finding one that appeals to the customer. Knowing the customer will help the seller better determine which close to use. Following are thirteen of the many low-risk closes available to a salesperson:

1. Backup or Alternate Vendor Close
2. Weighing or Ben Franklin Close
3. Financial Balance Sheet Close
4. Loaded Yes Close
5. Minor Point Close
6. Five Yeses Close
7. Puppy Dog Close
8. Trial-Order Close
9. Trial-Offer Close

10. Preference Close
11. Add-on Close
12. Choice Close
13. Self Close

1. The Backup or Alternate Vendor Close

The Backup or Alternate Vendor Close is a low-risk close that can be used as an indirect or a direct close. In this technique the buyer is prompted to make a purchase in the interest of having a second or alternate supplier. This close is appropriate for both business-to-business and retail sales.

Most Effective Use of This Close

This close is most effective with prospects who are

- Security-minded.
- Insecure about their relationships with their present vendors.
- Uncertain of their present vendors' abilities to maintain satisfactory price levels, delivery terms, or future considerations.
- Dissatisfied with their current vendors or want to create some competition for their vendors.

When Not to Use This Close

A salesperson should avoid using this close when the prospect already has a satisfactory relationship with an alternate vendor.

Examples of the Backup or Alternate Vendor Close

- "Why don't you use us as a backup vendor?"
- "By using us as an alternate supplier, you're letting your present vendors know that they had better maintain their quality of service to you. When would you like to start with us?"
- "Using us as a backup supplier is like having a safety net. Don't you think this is a smart move?"

If the Buyer Replies in a Positive Way

The sale is successfully concluded and further confirmed through assumptive statements on the seller's part, such as

- "Fine. What type of initial order would you like to start with?"
- "Thank you for your confidence. Would you prefer beginning with a full order?"
- "Great. Then let's place an order for you right away."

If the Close Is Rejected

The salesperson can easily counter with

- "What prompts you to reject this idea?"
- "Is there something in your contract with your present vendor that limits your having an alternate supplier?"
- "Are you against this added security?"

These questions will encourage the prospect to reveal information that may have been previously withheld from the salesperson.

2. The Weighing or Ben Franklin Close

The Weighing or Ben Franklin Close is a low-risk indirect close. Through this technique the seller closes the prospect by pointing out that the advantages outweigh the disadvantages of buying and using the vendor's product or service. The salesperson must be certain to have more reasons for buying than the client might have for not buying.

Most Effective Use of This Close

This close is most effective when the prospect is encouraged to write down the pros and cons of making this purchase.

When Not to Use This Close

Salespeople should avoid using this close when

- There are unusually difficult time constraints.
- They do not know the benefits of their products or services well enough to discuss them with their prospects.

An Example of the Weighing or Ben Franklin Close

This example must be altered to address the selling situation and the prospect's personality.

> *Salesperson:* "Why don't we look at both sides of this question? Please help me. Do you have a piece of paper and a pen available?"

The salesperson pauses while the prospect gets materials.

> *Salesperson:* "Excellent. Please draw a line down the middle of the paper."

Again the seller pauses until the buyer has drawn the line and then continues.

> *Salesperson:* "Please title the left side *Liabilities* and the right side *Positive Reasons to Buy.*"

Note: Other words or phrases may serve individual situations better than liabilities or reasons to buy.

> *Salesperson:* "On the left side of the paper, write out the reasons you might choose not to make this purchase."

Time is given for the prospect to write out a few objections.

> *Salesperson:* "Now on the right side of the paper, please write out all the positive reasons for making this purchase."

The salesperson should assist the customer if any positive reasons have been overlooked. The seller and customer then compare the two sides.

If the Buyer Replies in a Positive Way

The seller verifies the successful completion of the sale by concluding with a statement such as

- "Fine. Then let's write up a request and get our operations people moving on this."
- "Great. Do you want your service to begin on Monday or Tuesday?"

If the Close Is Rejected

The salesperson can ask

- "What causes you to say no?"
- "Is there something that's still bothering you?"

The seller's objective in asking these questions is to keep the selling process open. After responding to the customer's needs, the salesperson should attempt to close again.

3. The Financial Balance Sheet Close

The Financial Balance Sheet Close is a low-risk indirect close. This technique calls for the seller to close the prospect by pointing out the financial advantages and benefits of buying the salesperson's products or services. The seller may also compare his or her financial offer with the competition's.

Most Effective Use of This Close

This close is most effective when (as in the weighing close) the seller involves the customer in a writing exercise. The salesperson must know the competition's prices and the customer costs (including, where appropriate, financing, warehousing, and delivery costs) in order to implement this close effectively.

When Not to Use This Close

A salesperson should avoid using this close when

- The seller is not familiar with the financial aspects of the transaction.
- The prospect does not care about or have a vested interest in what the price is.

An Example of the Financial Balance Sheet Close

This example must be altered to address the selling situation and the prospect's personality.

> *Salesperson:* "Let's estimate the cost of buying this service from your present suppliers and

> then compare it with the investment your company would make with us."

The seller gives the prospect the figures involved or asks the buyer to estimate the figures. The salesperson also asks the prospect to write those figures on the paper. Getting the prospect involved by writing is critical to the success of this type of close. The customer's active participation in the closing process is a positive indication that she or he is interested in the sale. Subconsciously the prospect may even be weighing the wisdom of making the purchase. At this point the prospect is moving nearer to the closing stage.

If the Buyer Replies in a Positive Way

The salesperson might conclude the sale by asking further closing questions, such as

- "Would you prefer to have our service people perform the maintenance, or would you rather we train your service people?"
- "When is a better time to start the program, Friday or Monday?"
- "Do you prefer taking care of this by check or cash?"

If the Buyer Is Unwilling to Conduct a Cost Review

The salesperson should ask the customer one of the following questions:

- "Why do you object?"
- "Is there something wrong?"
- "Are you interested in getting the highest return from your investment?"

The seller must carefully pose these questions to the prospect. One's tone of voice and inflection must be in harmony with the presentation. The objective is to help, not challenge, the buyer.

If the Close Is Rejected After the Cost Review

The salesperson should openly and respectfully discuss the figures just calculated, as follows:

- "Do the figures seem reasonable?"
- "Do you think our estimates are accurate?"
- "How do these figures compare with your budget?"
- "How do these figures compare with our competition's proposals?"

These, plus other questions, will encourage the customer to clarify whatever objections might remain. This will give the salesperson more information and time with which to better answer the customer's needs. The seller should then attempt to close again.

4. The Loaded Yes Close

The Loaded Yes Close is a low-risk direct close. In this technique the seller phrases the closing question in such a way that the buyer must say yes.

Most Effective Use of This Close

This close is most effective when the seller knows the buyer well enough to accurately anticipate the buyer's response to such a close.

When Not to Use This Close

A salesperson should avoid using this close if

- Unsure of what to do should the customer say *yes*.
- Fearful that the prospect's answer will be negative.

Examples of the Loaded Yes Close

- "You do want an automobile with plenty of head room, don't you?"
- "This is the style you want, isn't it?"
- "This is what you wanted, isn't it?"

If the Buyer Replies in a Positive Way

The seller can then reply with

- "Would you prefer it in red or blue?"
- "Then when would you like it delivered, on Friday or Monday?"
- "Is it still what you want, or were you thinking of one of the better models?"

If the Close Is Rejected

The salesperson will have to tactfully deal with the customer by asking

- "Should we look at a different model?"
- "What would you prefer instead of this one?"
- "Would you prefer one of our other models?"

These types of questions may help the seller develop a new closing approach with the prospect.

5. The Minor Point Close

The Minor Point Close is a low-risk indirect close. In this technique the salesperson seeks a prospect's approval on a minor point and then proceeds to close by following it up with an Assumptive Close.

Most Effective Use of This Close

This close is most effective when the prospect is extremely interested in or excited about the product or service.

When Not to Use This Close

A salesperson should avoid using this close when

- The prospect is disinterested in the product or service.
- The prospect is hostile or negative toward the product, service, or salesperson.

Examples of the Minor Point Close

- *Salesperson:* "Did you say Friday was a good delivery day?"

  Prospect: "Yes."

  Salesperson: "Then we will deliver it before noon."

- *Salesperson:* "Do you think the red one would fit your color scheme?"

  Prospect: "Yes, it does."

  Salesperson: "Excellent, then we will wrap that one up."

Note: A Choice Close can also be a Minor Point Close.

If the Buyer Replies in a Positive Way

The seller then responds with

- "Then let's formalize our agreement!"
- "Good. I'll note that in our contract."

If the Close Is Rejected

The salesperson should quickly ask

- "How can we rectify that issue?"
- "What would you like us to do about it?"

The seller should remain positive throughout the entire process and look for new closing opportunities.

6. The Five Yeses Close

The Five Yeses Close is a low-risk direct close. This close involves four questions that rely on data previously discussed during the sales call. All the questions must call for a *yes* answer from the prospect. The fifth question is the closing question.

Most Effective Use of This Close

This close is most effective for the seller who carefully listens and accurately notes the prospect's interests and needs.

When Not to Use This Close

A salesperson should avoid using this close if

- Unsure of what the closing question or statement should be.
- Uncertain of the prospect's answers to the first four questions.

An Example of the Five Yeses Close

This example must be altered to address the selling situation and the prospect's personality.

Salesperson: "You did say you like our guarantee?"

Prospect: "Yes."

Salesperson: "You are satisfied with our servicing arrangements?"

Prospect: "Yes."

Salesperson: "And our price sounds reasonable?"

Prospect: "Yes."

Salesperson: "You wanted two cases of oil?"

Prospect: "Yes."

Salesperson: "And tomorrow is a good delivery day?"

Prospect: "Yes."

If the Buyer Replies in a Positive Way

The seller then responds with

- "We will process your order right away!"
- "Thank you."

If the Close Is Rejected

The salesperson should quickly ask, "Is there something I missed?" If the customer responds with an unfilled need, the seller will have to satisfy that need in order to continue the closing process. Once the need is satisfied, the seller should use another trial close.

7. The Puppy Dog Close

The Puppy Dog Close is a low-risk direct close. This technique calls for closing a prospect by lending him or her products or services on a trial basis (normally at no charge to the prospect). The term for this close comes from the pet shop business. Pet shop owners know that once a puppy dog is taken home on a trial basis it is rarely returned. The same holds true for products and services. Once they become part of a household or organization, they too are rarely returned.

Most Effective Use of This Close

This close is most effective when the prospect is sincerely interested in the product or service offered.

When Not to Use This Close

Salespeople should avoid using this close when

- They know that their products or services will not satisfy their prospects' needs.
- Their prospects are only interested in the free offering and show no interest in making a purchase regardless of the products' or services' quality, capabilities, or value.

Examples of the Puppy Dog Close

- "Why don't you take one of our copiers with you for one week, and see if it meets your needs better than the one you're currently using?"
- "We'll send you a month's free subscription to our paper. At the end of the month we'll call to see if you'd like to continue."

If the Buyer Replies in a Positive Way

The salesperson responds with

- "Excellent. We'll send you a unit tomorrow."
- "Fine. We'll begin the service right away."

If the Close Is Rejected

The salesperson can answer each as follows:

- "There's no cost or obligation to you or your organization. Besides, it could save you a lot of money if you do decide to keep it. You have everything to gain and nothing to lose."
- "There's no charge to you. Simply enjoy it. All you have to do is just say no at any time and the paper stops coming to your door. But say yes and you'll have the convenience of having it delivered to your home every day at a great savings over the newsstand cost. What do you have to lose?"

These statements and questions are designed to help the seller continue the closing process despite the prospect's earlier rebuffs.

8. The Trial-Order Close

The Trial-Order Close is a low-risk direct close. In this close the buyer is encouraged to make a test purchase to evaluate the item's value or the vendor's ability to perform.

Note: This close should not be confused with the Trial Close or the Trial-Offer Close, as they are separate activities.

Most Effective Use of This Close

This close is most effective with customers who are

- Not willing to make long-term commitments.
- Uncertain of the quality, value, or durability of the purchase.
- Interested but not convinced that they should be making a purchase.

When Not to Use This Close

A salesperson should avoid using this close when the prospect appears to be willing to make a purchase without the added incentive of a trial period or trial order.

Examples of the Trial-Order Close

- "Start our service on Monday. If you're dissatisfied for any reason you can cancel any time within thirty days and you'll be billed nothing. Is Monday a good day for you?"
- "Why don't you give me a trial order so I can prove my company's ability to take care of your needs?"

If the Buyer Replies in a Positive Way

If the sale is successfully concluded, the seller should ask or suggest something like the following:

- "Fine. We'll begin on Monday."
- "Excellent. Do you want to keep the order the size we originally discussed, or would you prefer to increase it?"

If the Close Is Rejected

The salesperson can reply with

- "If Monday isn't a good day, which day would you prefer?"
- "If you can't give us an order today, when would be a better time for us to start our relationship?"

These questions will help the seller keep the selling process open.

9. The Trial-Offer Close

The Trial-Offer Close is a low-risk direct close. In this close the buyer is encouraged to take advantage of a temporary offer of the product or service. A Trial-Offer Close

- Is subject to change without notice.
- Introduces the product or service to a new prospect (or a new product or service to an existing or past customer).
- Encourages a prospect to test-purchase a product or service (to demonstrate an item's or vendor's ability to perform as promised).

Note: This close should not be confused with the Trial Close or the Trial-Order Close, as they all differ.

Most Effective Use of This Close

This close is most effective with customers who are

- Not willing to make long-term commitments.
- Uncertain of the quality, value, or durability of the purchase.

- Interested but not convinced that they should be making a purchase.

When Not to Use This Close

A salesperson should avoid using this close when the prospect appears willing to make a purchase without the added incentive of a trial offer.

Examples of the Trial-Offer Close

- "Try our service for seven days at our discounted price. We'll phone you at the end of the trial period. If you don't like it, we'll bill you only for what you have used. However, I believe you'll like it. In that case, just say 'Please continue the service.' We'll invoice you for the discounted trial program. After that, we'll invoice you at our regular rate. Does that sound reasonable to you?"

- "Try our product for thirty days free of charge. If you like it, keep it. We'll send the invoice by the thirty-fifth day. That invoice will be payable thirty days from the time you receive it. It's like getting over two months' interest-free use of our money. How do these two offers sound to you?"

If the Buyer Replies in a Positive Way

If the sale is successfully concluded, the seller should ask or suggest the following:

- "Great. Would you like us to start the service today or tomorrow?"

- "Terrific. We'll send it out on Monday, if that's convenient for you."

If the Close Is Rejected

The salesperson can reply with

- "I'm sorry. Is there something I missed?"
- "Were you thinking of paying for it C.O.D.?"

These questions will help the seller keep the selling process open.

10. The Preference Close

The Preference Close is a low-risk indirect close. In this close the prospect is asked which product or service he or she prefers. Avoid offering more than three choices because this may confuse the prospect.

Most Effective Use of This Close

This close is most effective with customers who are uncertain of what they want. The Preference Close calls for an opinion rather than a decision and is therefore classified as a low-risk indirect close.

When Not to Use This Close

Salespeople should avoid using this close when they are

- Confused about closing the prospect.
- Unprepared to quickly follow up this close with a written or verbal contract.

Examples of the Preference Close

- "Would you prefer us to deliver your boxes on Monday or Tuesday?"
- "Would you prefer a credit plan or the use of cash?"

- "Would you prefer the larger or smaller model?" The word *prefer* sets up the close, as it implies acceptance or agreement by both parties.

If the Buyer Replies in a Positive Way

The sale is successfully concluded and further confirmed through assumptive statements on the seller's part, such as

- "Fine. Then expect our truck on Monday."
- "Excellent. I'll make that notation on your sales request."
- "Then we'll ship the smaller one out to you today. Is there anything else we might be able to help you with?"

If the Close Is Rejected

The salesperson can easily counter with

- "Is there some other day you were thinking of?"
- "Were you considering a layaway program or something else?"
- "Is there something wrong with these two items?"

These questions will help the seller search for new closing opportunities.

11. The Add-on Close

The Add-on Close is a low-risk direct close. Following a successful close, a second closing attempt is made to encourage the customer to buy more, in addition to the original purchase.

Most Effective Use of This Close

This close is most effective with customers who

- Have made a commitment to buy.
- Are agreeing with the seller's closing attempts.

When Not to Use This Close

A salesperson should avoid using this close with a prospect who has not committed to making a purchase.

Examples of the Add-on Close

- "I'll have your order ready tomorrow. Would you like to purchase a second model at this low figure?"
- "You've just saved yourself a lot of money. Would you like to increase your savings by increasing the order?"
- "We'll ship your request right away. What else would you like to order today?"

If the Buyer Replies in a Positive Way

The salesperson should reconfirm the close by offering other statements such as

- "Thank you. I'll initiate your second request right away."
- "Very good. I'm certain you'll enjoy the money you saved."
- "Would you like this order sent with the first one or shipped separately?"

If the Close Is Rejected

The salesperson can recover from an Add-on Close rejection by asking the customer another question, such as

- "Is there something else I can do for you today?"
- "Okay. Is there anything else you may need?"
- "Thank you. Is there anything else you would like to review with me?"

The seller should avoid asking these questions in a routine way. Furthermore, the salesperson should be as sincere as possible, since such questions can often cause buyers to rethink their actions. Sometimes this process causes the buyer to look at the seller's other products or services.

12. The Choice Close

The Choice Close is a low-risk indirect close. This is a selling technique that calls for the seller to close the sale by offering the prospect a choice among several items (colors, quantities, qualities, delivery dates, or price ranges, for example). Avoid offering more than three choices, because this may confuse the prospect. The Choice Close is simple and easy to use.

Most Effective Use of This Close

This close is most effective when

- The salesperson (offering two options) places the option favorable to the seller in the second position, since the second option is the one the customer most likely remembers and accepts.
- The salesperson (offering three options) places the option favorable to the seller in the second position,

since the middle choice is often thought of as the safest move.

This close is almost identical to the Preference Close described earlier in this chapter. The difference between the two is that the Choice Close uses a term other than "prefer" in calling for a buying decision.

When Not to Use This Close

Salespeople should avoid using this close when they are

- Confused as to how to close their prospects.
- Unprepared to quickly follow up this close with a written or verbal contract.

Examples of the Choice Close

- "Will you want one or two of these items?"
- "Which is better for your office, the red model or the brown?"
- "Would you want to pick up your dress on Tuesday or Wednesday?"

If the Buyer Replies in a Positive Way

The salesperson should reconfirm the close by offering other statements, such as:

- "Then I'll initiate your request today for two items."
- "The brown model is an excellent choice. Do you want to pay for this today or make a deposit?"
- "Good. I'll have your dress ready on Wednesday. Would you prefer to look at another dress or a blouse next?"

If the Close Is Rejected

The salesperson can easily recover from a Choice Close rejection by asking the customer another question, such as

- "Neither? Are you considering something else?"
- "Is there another color you prefer?"
- "What other day would you prefer?"

In many cases, other questions will follow these, giving the salesperson more information and time to better answer the customer's needs and to attempt to close again.

13. The Self Close

The Self Close is a low-risk indirect close. In this technique the seller encourages the prospect to close himself or herself.

Most Effective Use of This Close

This close is most effective when the seller is more of a consultant and a good listener than an overly aggressive salesperson. It is the most difficult close of all to engineer and much too lengthy to give an example of here. This type of selling calls for a high-level, professional rapport with the customer, as well as knowledge of the customer's problems. It calls for a problem-solving approach, knowing how to ask questions and allowing the client to solve the problem independently.

When Not to Use This Close

Salespeople should avoid using this close when they are

- Unsure of how to implement the Self Close process.
- Dealing with prospects who refuse to participate in the sale.

Examples of the Self Close

Because of the complexity and length of the Self Close, there are no typical examples of this process.

If the Buyer Replies in a Positive Way

The salesperson should reconfirm the close by offering other statements, such as

- "Then I'll initiate your request today."
- "Do you want to pay for this today or make a deposit?"

If the Close Is Rejected

If the Self Close is rejected, the seller should further explore the prospect's needs and trial close again through the use of a simpler close.

Chapter Summary

1. The **Backup** or **Alternate Vendor Close** (low-risk, direct or indirect, close)—The buyer is prompted to make a purchase in the interest of having a second or alternate supplier. This close is appropriate for both business-to-business and retail sales.

2. The **Weighing** or **Ben Franklin Close** (low-risk indirect close)—The seller closes the prospect by pointing out that the advantages outweigh the disadvantages of buying and using the vendor's product or service. The salesperson must be certain to have more reasons for buying than the client might have for not buying.

3. The **Financial Balance Sheet Close** (low-risk indirect close)—The seller closes the prospect by pointing out the financial advantages and benefits of

buying the salesperson's products or services. The seller may also compare his or her financial offer with the competition's.

4. The **Loaded Yes Close** (low-risk direct close)—The seller phrases the closing question in such a way that the buyer has to say *yes*.

5. The **Minor Point Close** (low-risk indirect close)— The salesperson seeks a prospect's approval on a minor point and then proceeds to close by following it up with an Assumptive Close.

6. The **Five Yeses Close** (low-risk direct close)—This close involves four questions that rely on data previously discussed during the sales call. All the questions must call for a *yes* answer from the prospect. The fifth question is the closing question.

7. The **Puppy Dog Close** (low-risk direct close)— This technique calls for closing a prospect by lending him or her products or services on a trial basis (normally at no charge to the prospect).

8. The **Trial-Order Close** (low-risk direct close)—The buyer is encouraged to make a test purchase to evaluate the item's value or the vendor's ability to perform.

9. The **Trial-Offer Close** (low-risk direct close)—The buyer is encouraged to take advantage of a temporary offer of the product or service. A Trial-Offer Close

   • Is subject to change without notice.

   • Introduces the product or service to a new prospect (or a new product or service to an existing or past customer).

- Encourages a prospect to test-purchase a product or service (to demonstrate an item's or vendor's ability to perform as promised).

10. The **Preference Close** (low-risk indirect close)— The prospect is asked which product or service he or she prefers. Avoid offering more than three choices because this may confuse the prospect.

11. The **Add-on Close** (low-risk direct close)—Following a successful close a second closing attempt is made to encourage the customer to buy more in addition to the original purchase.

12. The **Choice Close** (low-risk indirect close)—This calls for the seller to close the sale by offering the prospect a choice among several items (quantities, colors, qualities, delivery dates, or price ranges, for example). Avoid offering more than three choices, because this may confuse the prospect.

13. The **Self Close** (low-risk indirect close)—The seller encourages the prospect to close himself or herself.

4

THE HIGH-RISK CLOSES

Definitions and Models

Use high-risk closes sparingly and carefully.

"Of the five steps of the sale—greeting, warm-up, qualification, presentation and close—which is the most important?" I asked the classroom of thirty senior salespeople.

"They are equally important," one of the sellers in the front row responded rapidly. "If one of the five steps is not initiated professionally, it will throw off the rest."

I smiled but did not respond to her answer.

"That's not accurate," replied another. "I've seen salespeople do almost everything wrong and still close their deals. The only thing you have to do well is to close."

A few of the participants began scanning their notes for an answer.

"But if you fail to develop a personal rapport with the prospect through the warm-up step, your chances of closing diminish considerably," commented a person from the back of the room.

Several of the class members who could not answer the question began feeling rather awkward.

"It's the presentation," observed yet another sales veteran. "If you fail to make a presentation that appeals to the buyer's personality and needs, you can forget the close."

A few of the sellers began to snicker as if my query was a trick question.

Finally, one salesperson confidently stated with a smile, "The qualification step is the most important step of the sale."

"You're right," I answered. "The qualification is the most important step of the sale."

Before I could justify my remarks another participant shot back, "No, he's wrong. You can close a sale without qualifying the prospect thoroughly."

"You are also right," I stated.

By now many of the class members were confused by my last two statements, which seemed to conflict.

"I see what you mean," replied the participant who originally stated that the qualification is the most important step. "You really didn't contradict yourself as I first thought. You still maintain that the qualification step is the most important step, right?"

"Yes," I answered as the rest of the class attempted to understand what appeared to be a sort of riddle.

"And you can close without qualifying the account thoroughly," he went on.

"Yes. Poor qualifications occur all the time. Many salespeople don't know how to qualify their prospects," I continued.

"But without a well-developed qualification effort, the close is much more difficult to conclude successfully," he added.

"You're right again," I answered. "If you fail to qualify the client's needs well, you may make a poor presentation."

"Or misclose the customer," commented another seller.

"Like I did!" laughed another person. "I spent two hours with an account some years ago without qualifying her thoroughly. Boy, did I pay for that mistake. You see, I was trying to close a customer on $100,000 worth of business when she was only interested in a $100 service that my company no longer offered. I was embarrassed when after two hours she restated what she was interested in. Needless to say, no sale was made that day."

Several of the participants nodded their heads as if the same had happened to them.

"I've made similar mistakes," a salesperson in the back confessed. "Asking the right questions and listening are critical to making the right presentations and using the right closing questions."

"How can you make a professional presentation that's tailored to the prospect's needs if you don't fully understand the prospect's needs?" I asked. "The qualification step is that stage of the sale that allows you to gather information about the customer's needs, ideas, and preferences."

"So you tailor your presentation to the buyer's needs, as a result of what you discovered during the qualification step," one of the younger people stated.

"Correct," I answered. "If you don't qualify thoroughly, you may fail to make the right presentation and also fail to close effectively."

(Those readers who are interested in learning how to qualify their customers more effectively and more professionally should read my book *1st Impressions.*)

Poor qualification practices increase the chance for failure in closing, often compelling some sellers to attempt to use high-risk closes. This only causes the customer to further avoid making a positive buying decision.

Seven high-risk closes are covered in this chapter. These are closing statements and questions that may make buyers feel like sellers are pressuring them. Use these closes carefully. The term high risk is meant to imply that there is a strong probability of failure. Each of these closes has a purpose in the selling business. Many of you probably feel that you would never use high-risk closes. However, many do frequently use these closes in their nonbusiness-related communications.

Evaluating Your Closing Style
Part III—Closing Phrases You Tend to Use

Before you read further, you might want to assess your use of closing phrases. If you have not read the instructions that precede the self-assessment exercise in Chapter 2, you might read those sections at this time (*Evaluating Your Closing Style Part I—Attitude* and *Exercise Suggestions*).

Exercise
Closing Styles Study
Part III—Closing Phrases You Tend to Use

Instructions

Check the letter next to the answer that is most accurate. You may check a second option if a second answer also applies. For example:

    0. I like to close

          a. Rapidly

✓   b. In a subtle way

✓✓   c. After I get to know the prospect

In making your choices

- Do not mark any phrase you are uncertain of or that does not apply.
- Check the *Glossary* or *Index* for any word that is unfamiliar.
- Be as honest as possible and mark the way you actually perform or behave.

A continuation of the Closing Styles Study Exercise, this section begins with number 21.

21. Of these choices, I use this close or a similar one:
    a. "You're probably not interested in a high-quality buy anyhow."
    b. "Would you like three or four of these items?"
    c. "Can I send this one to you?"
    d. I use any of these closes whenever it is appropriate to do so.

22. Of these choices, I use this close or a similar one:
    a. "If we meet your needs, will you give us an order?"
    b. "If we meet your needs, will you consider giving us an order?"
    c. "The price is going up tomorrow. You'd better buy now."
    d. I use any of these closes whenever it is appropriate to do so.

23. Of these choices, I use this close or a similar one:
    a. "Would you like to make a purchase?"
    b. "Let's review the pros and cons of making this purchase."
    c. "You're probably not interested in a money-back offer."
    d. I use any of these closes whenever it is appropriate to do so.

24. Of these choices, I use this close or a similar one:
    a. "Buy it now. If you decide you don't want it, call me and cancel tomorrow."
    b. "You probably don't want to buy anything today, do you?"

    c. "Let's review the advantages and disadvantages of this purchase."

    d. I use any of these closes whenever it is appropriate to do so.

25. Of these choices, I use this close or a similar one:

    a. "If you don't decide now, you may not get the delivery you want."

    b. "Would you like three or four of these items?"

    c. "Can I send this one to you?"

    d. I use any of these closes whenever it is appropriate to do so.

26. Of these choices, I use this close or a similar one:

    a. "The price is going up tomorrow. You'd better buy now."

    b. "If we meet your terms, will you give us an order?"

    c. "Should we write up the order?"

    d. I use any of these closes whenever it is appropriate to do so.

27. Of these choices, I use this close or a similar one:

    a. "If I alter the terms, will you buy from me?"

    b. "You'd better buy now before we exhaust our supply of this unit."

    c. "Would you like to make a purchase?"

    d. I use any of these three closes whenever it is appropriate to do so.

28. I use

    a. High-risk closes most of the time.

    b. Low-risk closes most of the time.

    c. Both types of closes equally well and as needed.

29. I use indirect closes
    a. Only if my other closes fail.
    b. With ease in combination with my other closes.
    c. More regularly than any other type of close.

30. I use direct closes
    a. Very rarely.
    b. Regularly, regardless of the prospective buyer's personality.
    c. Easily, as needed, and especially with aggressive buyers.

Scoring
Closing Styles Study
Part III—Closing Phrases You Tend to Use

Legend

PO — Pressure-Oriented or Aggressive Closer
CA — Closure-Aversive or Noncloser
PS — Professional or Subtle Closer

Instructions

From the previous *Exercise,* circle the same letters below, including the score.

After completing this section, proceed to the *Score Box.* Make certain your answers reflect the way you actually interact with your prospects and customers.

21. Of these choices, I use this close or a similar one:
    a. PO
    b. PS
    c. CA
    d. PS

22. Of these choices, I use this close or a similar one:
    a. PS
    b. CA
    c. PO
    d. PS

23. Of these choices, I use this close or a similar one:
    a. CA
    b. PS
    c. PO
    d. PS

24. Of these choices, I use this close or a similar one:
    a. PO
    b. CA
    c. PS
    d. PS

25. Of these choices, I use this close or a similar one:
    a. PO
    b. PS
    c. CA
    d. PS

26. Of these choices, I use this close or a similar one:
    a. PO
    b. PS
    c. CA
    d. PS

27. Of these choices, I use this close or a similar one:
    a. PS
    b. PO
    c. CA
    d. PS

28. I use
    a. PO
    b. CA
    c. PS
29. I use indirect closes
    a. PO
    b. PS
    c. CA
30. I use direct closes
    a. CA
    b. PO
    c. PS

Score Box
Closing Styles Study
Part III—Closing Phrases You Tend to Use

Instructions

Each of your checked answers is worth ten points. Halve the value (five points each) wherever you have selected two answers under the same question. Total your score for each category and place it on the line to the right of the appropriate classification.

	Closing Tendency	Total Points
PO —	Pressure-Oriented Closer	_____
CA —	Closure-Aversive Closer	_____
PS —	Professional Closer	_____

Find your scores for each category (PO, CA, PS) on Table 4-1. If your total score for any category is 70 or 40, read both phrases (just above and below that score). The analysis is based solely on the accuracy of your selections. It reviews only the technical aspects of your closing practices.

If your responses are correct and your awareness is a reflection of your attitude toward closing, the assessment will be accurate. Other critical factors that impact your attitude (for example, appearance, body language, confidence, voice, product or service knowledge, and the sub-elements of the sale) are not factored into this study.

Table 4-1 Probable Tendencies Closing Styles Study Part III—Closing Phrases You Tend to Use		
PO Pressure-Oriented	CA Closure-Aversive	PS Professional
70 – 100 Points		
You get along best with people who like blunt, task-oriented sellers. You may tend to have confrontations with your peers, superiors, or customers.	Your closing phrases tend to be low-key and indirect. You may enjoy soft sales and customer and public relations positions more than hard sales.	You should be able to accurately anticipate your prospects' needs and vary your closes to enhance your position. You are flexible and responsive to others.
40 – 70 Points		
You can adjust your closing phrases to work well with dominant or passive prospects.	Unlike insensitive sellers, you use phrases that persuade sensitive prospects to buy.	You should be a good closer, but you need to learn how to capitalize on your closing abilities.
0 – 40 Points		
You sense others' needs and should be able to select the right phrases to win them over.	You are closing oriented and willing to close even under difficult circumstances.	A more professional and varied closing approach will improve your closing.

For a more personal and in-depth review, see the section at the back of this book titled *The Lizardy Associates Closing Styles (Complimentary) Analysis*. Regardless of how you scored, review the practices recommended in this book.

Look for those techniques that can help you, and put them to work as soon as possible.

High-Risk Closes

Salespeople need to be careful in using high-risk closes. These closes are presented for the purpose of teaching how to close. They also appear here because many experienced *buyers* use the very same selling techniques that salespeople employ to influence vendors to lower prices or increase benefits to the buyers (usually at no added cost). To use an old expression, forewarned is forearmed. The following are seven common high-risk closes:

1. Misstated Higher Quantity Close
2. Asking for the Order Close
3. Reverse Psychology Close
4. Intimidation Close
5. Assumptive Close
6. Guilt Close
7. Pity Close

Some high-risk closes are also considered to be overtly manipulative closes, such as

- Misstated Higher Quantity Close
- Reverse Psychology Close
- Intimidation Close
- Guilt Close
- Pity Close

In the hands of an unscrupulous individual, these closes are easily misused. Salespeople should be extremely careful how they use these techniques. Most of these closes are last-resort efforts. Their use should be reserved for prospects who are harming themselves, their families, their organizations, or their peers as a result of not making a buying decision.

While I do not endorse the use of some of these closes, I feel it is important that businesspeople be made aware of these techniques and their usage. Many of the people that sellers deal with do use these ploys.

There are also other closes that may or may not be overtly manipulative, depending on their use:

- Assumptive Close
- Five Yeses Close
- Loaded Yes Close
- Puppy Dog Close

1. The Misstated Higher Quantity Close

The Misstated Higher Quantity Close is a high-risk close that can be classified as direct or indirect, depending on usage. It is a manipulative closing ploy in which the seller purposely quotes a higher price (or larger volume) than the prospect originally indicated and attempts to close the prospect when the buyer corrects the seller. This close creates anxiety and causes the customer to

- Indicate some interest in what the seller is proposing.
- Disclose an intent to make a purchase.

Most Effective Use of This Close

Using this close sparingly is a wise policy. It is a high-power, trick close and is most effective with prospects who refuse to respond to general questions. The intent here is to get a response, period!

When Not to Use This Close

Salespeople should avoid using this close when

- High-power closes are inappropriate.
- They are dealing with sophisticated prospects.

Examples of the Misstated Higher Quantity Close

- "Did you say you needed four or forty?"
- "Did you want the $250 pair of shoes in brown or black?"

If the Buyer Replies in a Positive Way

The salesperson should then respond

- "I will get the four dozen to you as soon as possible."
- "I can verify that we have the color you want and get back to you this afternoon."

If the Close Is Rejected

The salesperson can always respond with

- "Oh, I'm sorry, I thought you were ready to make a decision."
- "Didn't you say you wanted to make a purchase today?"
- "Oh, I thought we were just trying to make a decision on color."

This allows the seller to keep the selling process open. The salesperson may also gather new information dealing with the prospect's concerns. Through this process the seller also may be able to satisfy the prospect's concerns, thereby developing the opportunity for a new closing situation.

2. The Asking for the Order Close

The Asking for the Order Close is a high-risk direct close. In this closing technique the seller bluntly asks the buyer if he or she would like to make a purchase. Since it is an aggressive close, it can easily precipitate a defensive or negative response from the prospect. Direct closes are effective with only a limited number of customers. This type of close lacks any creative attempt by the salesperson to bring closure since it is a simple, direct question. Many sellers overuse this close and as a result lose far more sales than they realize.

Most Effective Use of This Close

This close is most effective when the seller and buyer have a friendly, open, and trusting relationship in which bluntness is not considered to be impolite or aggressive.

When Not to Use This Close

Salespeople should avoid using this close when

- More effective and more creative ways of closing their prospects are available.
- They are uncertain about what positive things to say or do should their prospects say no.

Examples of the Asking for the Order Close

- "Have you decided to buy from us?"
- "Does that mean you want to buy one?"
- "Would you like to buy it?"

If the Buyer Replies in a Positive Way

Once the sale is complete, the seller can finalize the details by asking

- "How many would you like?"
- "Excellent. When do you want it delivered?"
- "Is your company going to pay for it now or on delivery?"

If the Close Is Rejected

The likelihood of rejection is higher with this close than with a lower risk and more creative close. If the close is rejected, the salesperson must move quickly to handle the prospect's rebuff. The salesperson will have to ask other questions that encourage the customer to clarify the objections and needs. The seller's questions may sound like these:

- "What causes you to say no?"
- "Why not?"
- "Is there something you don't like about it?"

Being prepared and asking such questions will help the salesperson gather more information. It will also give the seller time to better answer the customer's needs and then attempt to close again.

3. The Reverse Psychology Close

The Reverse Psychology Close is a high-risk indirect close. In this close the seller overstates the opposite of what the prospect desires or expects in an attempt to close the prospect. It is a dangerous, high-risk close and can easily backfire. An intelligent customer could be offended by the use of this technique, since it is more associated with child psychology than it is with the business world. The Reverse Psychology Close is viewed by many sales trainers as more of a ploy than a close.

Most Effective Use of This Close

This close is most effective when dealing with customers who are susceptible to basic confrontation-oriented ploys.

When Not to Use This Close

Salespeople should avoid using this close when

- They are dealing with intelligent people.
- This negative approach is certain to end the seller's chances of making a sale.

Examples of the Reverse Psychology Close

- "You probably don't care about the special services we offer, do you?"
- "You're probably not interested in a product that could save you money, are you?"

If the Buyer Replies in a Positive Way

The seller can then proceed with

- "I'm glad to hear that you do care. Would you prefer a one-year or a two-year maintenance policy?"
- "It's good to hear that you are interested in our product. Would you like one or two?"

If the Close Is Rejected

The salesperson must move quickly to handle the rebuff. After all, the seller called for rejection and the customer gave the salesperson exactly what was asked for.

- "I understand. If I could show you a way to save money with this plan, would you have an interest in reviewing it?"
- "That's okay. Let's look at a model that better fits your needs."

The initial phrase in each of these replies, "I understand" and "That's okay," allows the seller to build a sympathetic relationship with the prospect. The follow-up phrase gives the salesperson the opportunity to keep the selling process alive.

4. The Intimidation Close

The Intimidation Close is a high-risk close that can be classified as direct or indirect, depending on usage. It creates a sense or fear of loss if the prospect fails to make a purchase. This may include the loss of

- Convenient or rapid delivery.
- Product or service availability.
- Time, money (price advantage), or effort.
- Some advantage over the prospect's competition.
- A good (wise and timely) purchase, the loss of which might be later criticized as a mistake by the buyer's peers or superior(s).

Most Effective Use of This Close

This close is most effective when the prospect recognizes that the seller's observations are accurate and that the prospect risks a real and important loss if action is not taken right away.

When Not to Use This Close

Salespeople should avoid using this close when they

- Know that they are not honest with their prospects.
- Are relatively certain that their customers' reactions will be negative.

Examples of the Intimidation Close

- Regarding the loss of time, the salesperson might say, "If we don't write the order immediately, there will be a longer wait for delivery since the delivery department takes orders only once a week and today is the cut-off day."
- Regarding the loss of money, the salesperson might say, "Our rates will go up next month. Any delay will cost you money."
- Regarding the loss of making a good decision, the seller might say, "This is the last and most advanced model of its type. If you fail to buy it now, it may be gone when you come back. You'll lose the opportunity to make a good decision and a smart buy all at the same time."
- Regarding losing an advantage to a competitor, the seller might say, "Your competition is using this more advanced system right now. If you fail to act on it soon, you'll fall farther behind."
- Regarding a lack of action that might be viewed later as a mistake by others, the salesperson might say, "This is an opportune moment for you to act on this matter. If you fail to do so, your peers may take advantage of this mistake."

Few selling agents like to admit that this type of selling is called intimidation selling. Yet the seller's intent is to spur a positive buying decision from the prospect by creating a sense of loss on the customer's part if the customer does not make the purchase immediately.

If the Buyer Replies in a Positive Way

The seller must complete the closing process by reconfirming certain issues, for example:

- "Great. This will save you several weeks. I'll call the order in today!"
- "You've just saved yourself a lot of money. Would you like to increase your savings even more by increasing the size of the order?"
- "You've made the right decision. What terms would be better for you, cash or charge?"
- "Thank you. Then I'll get going on it right away!"
- "Do you want me to enter your request on Tuesday or Thursday?"

If the Close Is Rejected

The salesperson has several ways of responding when the customer rejects the Intimidation Close. For example:

- Regarding the loss of time, the seller can respond with "Are you certain that you can afford the time differential when we could avoid that loss right now?"

The seller is causing the prospect to reevaluate the rejection. The seller is also attempting to reclose the prospect.

- Regarding the loss of money, the salesperson may respond with

    "Is the difference in costs important to you?"

    "Isn't the savings worth making your move now?"

These types of questions help the seller determine how much thought the prospect has invested in the analysis of the situation.

- Regarding the loss of making a good decision, the salesperson could respond with "What's stopping you from making the best move right now?"

The intent of this reply is to encourage prospects to reevaluate their decisions.

- Regarding the loss of an advantage to the competition, the salesperson can respond with "Is this possible loss of an advantage to your competition meaningful?"

The purpose of this question is to cause the prospect to evaluate what losses may be suffered as a result of not making the purchase.

- Regarding a lack of action that might be viewed later as a mistake by others, the salesperson may say, "Unfortunately for you, you have too much visibility. One mistake and your adversaries may try to take advantage of you. It's important that you make a good decision today."

These statements cause the prospect to take a larger view of the consequences of the decision not to buy.

5. The Assumptive Close

The Assumptive Close is a high-risk direct close. In this closing technique the seller assumes the prospect wants to make a purchase.

Most Effective Use of This Close

This close is most effective when dealing with an assertive prospect who is not annoyed by an assertive salesperson.

When Not to Use This Close

A salesperson should avoid using this close if he or she is

- Uncertain of what to do next.
- Unable to quickly prepare a written or verbal contract.

Examples of the Assumptive Close

- "We'll deliver your refrigerator on Monday."
- "Tell your loading dock people that we'll send four boxes."
- "What purchase order number do you want to assign to this order?"

The seller must be prepared to handle negative responses. This type of close is not for clients who are easily overwhelmed or who have the tendency to cancel orders the next day. This is considered a high-power close, but if handled tactfully it can be highly effective.

If the Buyer Replies in a Positive Way

The salesperson's next comments should respond positively to keep the flow of the closing process going.

- "Would you prefer a morning or afternoon delivery?"
- "I'm certain you'll find this product will do a much better job for you."
- "Fine. You can expect a Monday delivery."

If the Close Is Rejected

The salesperson must evaluate the customer's personality and respond accordingly. The following responses are usually safe with all types of customers:

- "Is there something wrong?"
- "Did I misinterpret your direction?"
- "I'm sorry. I thought you were ready to place an order."

These questions will help the seller better understand the prospect's direction. They can also help the seller overcome any hidden objections the customer may have.

6. The Guilt Close

The Guilt Close is a high-risk close that can be classified as direct or indirect, depending on usage. It is also a manipulative closing ploy in which the seller uses guilt in an effort to force the prospect into making a buying decision.

Most Effective Use of This Close

This close is most effective with prospects who are susceptible to feelings of guilt. The salesperson may appeal to the client's sense of personal obligations, duty, loyalty, fairness, or understanding.

When Not to Use This Close

A salesperson should avoid using this close when

- More positive closes are available.
- Dealing with a sophisticated prospect.
- Dealing with a customer who does not care about the seller's needs.

Examples of the Guilt Close

- "How would you feel if you failed to make this purchase and something went wrong as a result?"
- "Don't you owe this to your family (or employees/organization)?"
- "We've been friends for a long time—how could you turn me away now?"

If the Buyer Replies in a Positive Way

The salesperson should then respond

- "You've made a good decision. I'll process your request right away."
- "You can rest easy now that you've protected your family (or employees/organization)."
- "You're a good friend. I knew you wouldn't let me down. I'll send in your order immediately!"

If the Close Is Rejected

The salesperson can always respond with

- "I'm most concerned with your best interests and would hate to see you make this mistake—especially if something went wrong."
- "If something does go wrong, what will you tell your family (or employees/organization)?"
- "After all I've done for you, how could you do this to me? This allows the seller to keep the selling process open.

7. The Pity Close

The Pity Close is a high-risk direct close. It is a closing statement or question in which the seller manipulates the buyer's emotions (compassion, sensitivities, sympathies, tenderness) in an attempt to close the prospect.

Most Effective Use of This Close

This close is most effective with prospects who are susceptible to feelings of pity toward others.

When Not to Use This Close

A salesperson should avoid using this close when

- More positive closes are available.
- Dealing with a sophisticated prospect.
- Dealing with a customer who does not care about the seller's needs.

Examples of the Pity Close

- "I know my superiors will be extremely upset with me if you allow this one occurrence to ruin what has been a good working relationship all these years. What if I personally oversee your next shipment on Monday?"
- "I'm a new salesperson with the company, and gaining your business would be a tremendous boost to my career. I would really appreciate your help in getting this order, and you can be sure that I'll do everything possible to satisfy your needs."

If the Buyer Replies in a Positive Way

The seller adds

- "Thank you. I'll get started on it right away!"

- "I sincerely appreciate your sense of fairness. If you like, I'll be in contact with you through every step of the transaction."

If the Close Is Rejected

The salesperson has little maneuvering room as a result of a rebuff at a personal level. The Pity Close forces the seller to continue trying to appeal on an emotional level until the closing approach can be altered. Using humor to lessen the impact of this close helps both prospect and seller.

Chapter Summary

1. The **Misstated Higher Quantity Close** (high-risk close that can be viewed as direct or indirect, depending on its usage)—This is a manipulative closing ploy in which the seller purposely quotes a higher price (or larger volume) than the prospect originally indicated and attempts to close the prospect when the buyer corrects the seller.

2. The **Asking for the Order Close** (high-risk direct close)—The seller bluntly asks the buyer if he or she would like to make a purchase.

3. The **Reverse Psychology Close** (high-risk indirect close)—The seller overstates the opposite of what the prospect desires or expects in an attempt to close the buyer.

4. The **Intimidation Close** (high-risk close that can be classified as direct or indirect, depending on usage)—It creates a sense or fear of loss if the prospect fails to make a purchase, such as the loss of

   - Convenient or rapid delivery.
   - Product or service availability.

- Time, money (price advantage), or effort.
- An advantage over the prospect's competition.
- A good (wise and timely) purchase, the loss of which might be later criticized as a mistake by the buyer's peers or superior(s).

5. The **Assumptive Close** (high-risk direct close)—The seller assumes the prospect wants to make a purchase.

6. The **Guilt Close** (high-risk close, can be used as a direct or indirect close)—It is also a manipulative closing ploy in which the salesperson uses guilt in an effort to force the prospect into making a buying decision.

7. The **Pity Close** (high-risk direct close)—It is a closing statement or question in which the seller manipulates the buyer's emotions (compassion, sensitivities, sympathies, tenderness) in an attempt to close the prospect.

5

CLOSES THAT CAN BE CONSIDERED AS HIGH- OR LOW-RISK

Definitions and Models

There are two legitimate reasons for a seller
failing to close successfully:
(1) The prospect does not need the product or service.
(2) The prospect cannot afford, or finance, the purchase.

"Hello," the man at the door sang enthusiastically. "I'm conducting a survey for my company."

"Ah, good," I responded.

He smiled at my reply but was shocked when I asked, "What are you selling?"

"Nothing," he insisted. "This is just a survey."

I'm certain he's selling something like encyclopedias or magazine subscriptions, I thought.

"I guess you'd like to come inside and ask me a few questions?" I replied.

"How did you know?" he asked.

"I've met survey people in the past. Before you come in, I must warn you that I'm not about to buy anything."

"That's good, because I'm not selling anything," he stressed.

Within a few minutes it became obvious that he was selling encyclopedias. He was well-trained, systematic, and disciplined. Throughout the evening he attempted to get me to buy a set of his books. By the end of his presentation he had the floor covered with his most expensive maps, diagrams, and books. I was surrounded, having no place to step without marring one of his elaborate, full-color illustrations. I was soon to realize that I was dealing with one of the most persistent salespeople I had ever met.

"Well, let's write up a set of encyclopedias," he suggested boldly with a smile.

Assumptive Close, I thought as I replied, "I told you at the beginning, I'm not buying anything."

"Would you like to buy a set of encyclopedias to-night?" he asked.

Direct Close. He is asking for the order.

"No, thank you," I replied.

"Why is that?"

Now he is forcing me to justify and qualify my objection.

"I don't need a set of encyclopedias," I answered.

"Let's weigh the pros and cons here," he suggested. "Do you have a sheet of paper so that we can evaluate this challenge logically?"

The Weighing Close, plus he is trying to appeal to my sense of logic.

"No, thank you," I replied quickly.

"Would you like to buy our entire set tonight or purchase one book a month for the next thirty months?"

Choice Close.

"Neither."

"If I could show you a way of owning these books with little or no cost to you, would you be interested in purchasing them?"

Conditional Close, I thought as I remained silent.

"Let's take a look at how we could save you money through our special sale." With that, he reached for a pen to jot down several figures for me.

Financial Balance Sheet Close, I mused. Again I remained silent.

Breaking the silence, he said, "As I mentioned earlier, this set is on sale for a very limited time only. Don't you want to buy now and save yourself the costly increase you'll be facing if you don't act right away?"

Intimidation Close. He must know every close in the book, I marveled in silence and finally stated, "Money is not the problem here. I'm just not interested."

"Even if the set doesn't cost you a dime?"

Loaded Yes Close. He doesn't expect me to answer.

"Why don't you try our set free of charge for a week?"

Puppy Dog Close.

"I won't be home this week," I answered honestly.

"Next week then."

A combination of the Puppy Dog and Assumptive Closes.

"I'm really not interested," I stated softly.

"Wouldn't you like one of these fine-looking sets to adorn your beautiful home?" he asked.

Minor Point Close.

He continued with, "Just think how your friends will envy you as they see these fine books in your living room."

I remained silent.

"Do you have children, sir?"

"Yes," I mumbled. "A baby boy."

"You probably wouldn't want your son to be the head of his class anyway."

Reverse Psychology Close. What a dangerous tactic to use.

"You mean you would deprive your son of an education?" he replied.

Guilt Close.

"All of our public libraries have encyclopedias," I said.

"Sir, do you know your neighbors next door?"

Now he is going to use a Third-Party Reference Close.

"Yes."

"What do you think of them?"

He is prequalifying my opinion of my neighbors.

"Splendid people. The best neighbors we've ever had. Finest immigrants to this country I've ever met."

"Then their opinion matters to you."

"On some matters, yes."

"Well, they bought a set of encyclopedias from me last night."

An inferred close using peer pressure to engineer an agreement from me.

"You must be a wonderful salesperson," I replied with a smile.

"Why is that?" he asked.

"Neither one can read English."

With that, the salesperson finally realized that he could not make a sale and left. What he failed to acknowledge during most of our conversation was that I did not have a need for his product. There are two legitimate reasons for failing to close a transaction:

1. The prospect does not need the product or service.

2. The customer cannot afford to buy or finance the purchase.

The encyclopedia seller was polite, persistent, and professional throughout his presentation. He employed a variety of closes in his attempts to complete his transaction. This chapter examines three closes, two of which the seller used. These three closes can be classified as either high- or low-risk closes, depending on their use.

Evaluating Your Closing Style
Part IV—Closing Classifications
You Most Rely On

Before you read further, you might want to participate in the following closing style exercise, which deals with the types of closes you tend to use. If you have not read the instructions that precede the self-assessment exercise in Chapter 2, you might read those sections at this time (*Evaluating Your Closing Styles Part I—Implementation* and *Exercise Suggestions*).

Exercise
Closing Styles Study
Part IV—Closing Classifications
You Most Rely On

Instructions

Check the letter next to the answer that is most accurate. You may check a second option if a second answer also applies. For example:

  0. I like to close
- a. Rapidly
- ✓ b. In a subtle way
- ✓✓ c. After I get to know the prospect

In making your choices

- Do not mark any phrase you are uncertain of or that does not apply.

- Check the *Glossary* or *Index* for any word that is unfamiliar.

- Be as honest as possible and mark the way you actually perform or behave.

A continuation of the Closing Styles Study Exercise, this section begins with number 31.

  31. Of these choices, I use this close or a similar one:
- a. Asking for the Order Close.
- b. Assumptive Close.
- c. Choice Close.
- d. I use each of these closes easily and comfortably.

32. Of these choices, I use this close or a similar one:
    a. Reverse Psychology Close.
    b. Preference Close.
    c. I use each of these closes easily and comfortably.
    d. I don't close, I wait for my prospects to tell me when they are ready to buy.

33. Of these choices, I use this close or a similar one:
    a. Barter or Conditional Close.
    b. Guilt Close.
    c. I use each of these closes easily and comfortably.
    d. I don't close, I wait for my prospects to tell me when they are ready to buy.

34. Of these choices, I use this close or a similar one:
    a. Weighing or Ben Franklin Close.
    b. Intimidation Close.
    c. Pity Close.
    d. I use each of these closes easily and comfortably.

35. Of these choices, I use this close or a similar one:
    a. Third-Party Reference Close.
    b. Higher Reference Close.
    c. Asking for the Order Close.
    d. I use all three closes easily.

36. Of these choices, I use this close or a similar one:
    a. Pity Close.
    b. Self Close.
    c. Misstated Higher Quantity Close.
    d. I use all three closes easily.

37. Of these choices, I use this close or a similar one:
    a. Minor Point Close.
    b. Reverse Psychology Close.
    c. I use both closes easily.

    d. I don't close, I wait for my prospects to tell me when they are ready to buy.

38. Of these choices, I use this close or a similar one:

    a. Intimidation Close.

    b. Weighing or Ben Franklin Close.

    c. I use both closes easily.

    d. I don't close, I wait for my prospects to tell me when they are ready to buy.

39. Of these choices, I use this closing approach the most:

    a. As many closes as possible on each sales call.

    b. A combination of timely closes.

    c. Closing in response to the prospect's buying signals.

    d. I don't close, I wait for my prospects to tell me when they are ready to buy.

40. I would describe my closing habits as

    a. Tenacious, overt, and spontaneous.

    b. Persistent, subtle, and premeditated.

    c. Indirect, casual, and unplanned.

    d. Dependent on the prospect's needs and their personality.

Scoring
Closing Styles Study
Part IV—Closing Classifications
You Most Rely On

Legend

    PO — Pressure-Oriented or Aggressive Closer

    CA — Closure-Aversive or Noncloser

    PS — Professional or Subtle Closer

Instructions

From the previous *Exercise,* circle the same letters below, including the score.

After completing this section, proceed to the *Score Box.* Make certain your answers reflect the way you actually interact with your prospects and customers.

31. Of these choices, I use this close or a similar one:
    a. CA
    b. PO
    c. PS
    d. PS

32. Of these choices, I use this close or a similar one:
    a. PO
    b. PS
    c. PS
    d. CA

33. Of these choices, I use this close or a similar one:
    a. PS
    b. PO
    c. PS
    d. CA

34. Of these choices, I use this close or a similar one:
    a. PS
    b. PO
    c. CA
    d. PS

35. Of these choices, I use this close or a similar one:
    a. PS
    b. PO
    c. CA
    d. PS

36. Of these choices, I use this close or a similar one:
    a. CA
    b. PS
    c. PO
    d. PS

37. Of these choices, I use this close or a similar one:
    a. PS
    b. PO
    c. PS
    d. CA

38. Of these choices, I use this close or a similar one:
    a. PO
    b. PS
    c. PS
    d. CA

39. Of these choices, I use this closing approach the most:
    a. PO
    b. PS
    c. PS
    d. CA

40. I would describe my closing habits as:
    a. PO
    b. PS
    c. CA
    d. PS

Score Box
Closing Styles Study
Part IV—Closing Classifications
You Most Rely On

Instructions

Each of your checked answers is worth ten points. Halve the value (five points each) wherever you have selected two answers under the same question. Total your score for each category and place it on the line to the right of the appropriate classification.

	Closing Tendency	Total Points
PO —	Pressure-Oriented Closer	_____
CA —	Closure-Aversive Closer	_____
PS —	Professional Closer	_____

Find your scores for each category (PO, CA, PS) on Table 5-1. If your total score for any category is 70 or 40, read both phrases (just above and below that score). The analysis is based solely on the accuracy of your selections. It reviews only the technical aspects of your closing practices.

If your responses are correct and your awareness is a reflection of your attitude toward closing, the assessment will be accurate. Other critical factors that impact your attitude (for example, appearance, body language, confidence, voice, product or service knowledge, and the sub-elements of the sale) are not factored into this study.

Table 5-1 Probable Tendencies Closing Styles Study Part IV—Closing Classifications You Most Rely On		
PO Pressure-Oriented	CA Closure-Aversive	PS Professional
70 – 100 Points		
You use high-risk direct closes. You are independent and never seek approval for your conduct from your peers; rarely do you seek it from your superiors.	You dislike those who "throw their weight around." You close when you feel that the rewards are worth the effort and when it is *safe* for you to close.	You should be able to use a variety of closes with ease, as your closing awareness is exceptional. You can deal well with difficult prospects or customers.
40 – 70 Points		
As a closer, you are a calculated risk-taker. You will become a better seller if you listen more carefully to others.	You tend to use indirect and low-risk closes. You know the importance of tact and are able to get along with others.	Your prospects and customers like your responsiveness and closing style. Keep focused on satisfying their needs.
0 – 40 Points		
You can adjust your level of assertiveness to fit the situation. You sometimes "bend over backward" to help your customer.	You react rapidly to others. Take care not to overreact to a hostile prospect's objections. Also, listen carefully for buying signals.	You may occasionally fail to adjust your closing style to meet your prospects' needs, which affects your closing consistency.

For a more personal and in-depth review, see the section at the back of this book titled *The Lizardy Associates Closing Styles (Complimentary) Analysis*. Regardless of how you scored, review the practices recommended in this book. Look for those techniques that can help you, and put them to work as soon as possible.

Developing a Composite of Your Closing Style

If you are interested in developing a composite view of your closing style, total your scores from each part of the *Closing Styles Study* and divide by four. After arriving at that final score, reread the analysis in the sections that follow each exercise as they apply to your new score. Some participants will find that their overall score is similar to their four scores, while others will find some conflict in the way they scored. Such conflicts reveal an inconsistency in the way these people close.

High- or Low-Risk Closes

The following are three closes that can be considered as either high- or low-risk:

1. Higher Reference Close
2. Conditional or Barter Close
3. Third-Party Reference Close

1. The Higher Reference Close

The Higher Reference Close can be classified as a high- or low-risk and a direct or indirect close, depending on its usage. The seller uses the name of (or comments from) a powerful or influential person within the prospect's organization in order to influence the prospect's buying decisions. A salesperson must take care not to use this close in an aggressive way. Any attempt to openly intimidate the prospect could backfire.

Before using such a method, the seller must prequalify the listener as to how the prospect feels about the higher reference (be it the prospect's boss or someone else higher in the organization). If a salesperson wants to use a low-risk question to prequalify the listener's opinion of the person's boss, the seller can ask, "Does your boss have a lot of experience in this area?"

If a salesperson has a good relationship with the prospect and is willing to use a high-risk question to prequalify the listener's opinion of the boss, the seller can ask

- "Does your boss have much influence in making this decision?"
- "How do you feel about your boss's opinion on this subject?"

Most Effective Use of This Close

This close is most effective when dealing with prospects who have positive attitudes about their superiors' opinions.

When Not to Use This Close

A salesperson should avoid using this close if he or she is

- Unaware of the prospect's opinion of the superior.
- Uncertain of how to tactfully introduce the higher reference's comments.
- Certain that the higher reference's comments will negatively influence the prospect.

Examples of the Higher Reference Close

- "Did you know that the president of your company likes our services?"
- "Did you know that your boss has a high regard for our company?"
- "Did you know that several of your managers have reviewed our proposal and feel positive about it?"

If the Buyer Replies in a Positive Way

The seller could complete the close by saying

- "Great. Would you prefer starting the service in May or June?"
- "Thank you. Have you considered what financial terms your company will be interested in?"
- "I'm glad to hear that you all agree. What's our next step?"

If the Close Is Rejected

The salesperson should drop the reference and go on with the presentation. Care and tact should be taken in offering a Higher Reference Close since can be also a high-risk close.

2. The Conditional or Barter Close

The Conditional or Barter Close can be classified as a high- or low-risk and as a direct or indirect close, depending on usage. In this close the seller offers the prospect something in exchange for the buyer's acceptance of the transaction. The word "if" normally appears as a part of this technique.

Most Effective Use of This Close

This close is most effective when dealing with a customer who enjoys bartering.

When Not to Use This Close

Salespeople should avoid using this close when

- They are dealing with customers who do not like bartering.
- There is nothing of real value (to their prospects) to barter with.

Examples of the Low-Risk Conditional or Barter Close

- "If we can improve our delivery time, *will you consider* giving us an order?"
- "If we drop our price, *will you think* about giving us the entire order?"
- "If I could assure you that you will be completely reimbursed if there is any kind of damage, *would you again review* our proposal?"

Examples of the High-Risk Conditional or Barter Close

- "If we can improve our delivery time, *will you give us* an order?"
- "If we drop our price, *will you give us* the entire order?"
- "If I could assure you that you'll be completely reimbursed should any damage occur, *would you* buy our products?"

If the Buyer Replies in a Positive Way

Regardless of the high- or low-risk tone, the seller should then reply with

- "Good. Can we count on your full order this week or next week?"
- "Thank you. I'll get started on it today."
- "Then let's get started on it."

If the Close Is Rejected

The salesperson can counter with

- "What can we do to get a larger share of your business?"
- "Why won't you give us the entire order?"
- "Why?"

These questions are designed to encourage the prospect to reveal information thus far hidden from the salesperson.

3. The Third-Party Reference Close

The Third-Party Reference Close can be classified as a high- or low-risk and as a direct or indirect close, depending on its usage. In this selling technique the seller attempts to close the prospect by citing examples of past or present customers who are satisfied or impressed with the seller's products or services.

This close is similar to the third-party close. Once again, the seller must prequalify the listener to ascertain how the prospect feels about the source. Big names, prestigious organizations, and trendsetters are often cited in this type of close. Third-party closes usually set up the close and are occasionally the actual or final closing vehicle.

Salespeople have to be careful not to use third-party references in an intimidating or bragging manner. Testimonial letters (letters attesting to the product or service quality and customer satisfaction) support this type of close.

Most Effective Use of This Close

This close is used most effectively when dealing with a prospect who holds the third-party reference's opinion in high regard.

When Not to Use This Close

A salesperson should avoid using this close when

- Unaware of the prospect's opinion or image of the third party.
- Uncertain of how to tactfully introduce the third party's comments.

Examples of the Low-Risk Third-Party Reference Close

- "Here's a letter from Company Y (company with high name recognition) stating that our product is the best they've ever purchased. *Shouldn't you consider using it as well?"*
- "The biggest names in the industry (here a few companies are named) purchase from us because we work hard to satisfy their needs. *Perhaps you too might think about using us as a vendor."*

Examples of the High-Risk Third-Party Reference Close

- "Here's a letter from Company Y (company with high name recognition) stating that our product is the best they've ever purchased. *Shouldn't you be buying from us as well?"*
- "The biggest names in the industry (here a few companies are named) purchase from us because

we work hard to satisfy their needs. *Perhaps you should be buying from us as well."*

If the Buyer Replies in a Positive Way

The seller then seeks more details.

- "I'm glad to hear you feel the same. What's the best way for us to proceed?"
- "Excellent. Once you begin using us as your vendor, you'll also discover why those companies have stayed with us over the years. Does your company have a buying cycle?"
- "That's excellent. Would you prefer beginning delivery on Friday of this week or next?"
- "We welcome and appreciate your business. Would you prefer our discussing the terms this morning or after lunch?"

If the Close Is Rejected

The salesperson should drop the reference and go on with the presentation.

Chapter Summary

1. The **Higher Reference Close** (can be classified as a high- or low-risk and as a direct or indirect close, depending on usage)—The seller uses the name of (or comments from) a powerful or influential person within the prospect's organization in order to influence the prospect's buying decisions.

2. The **Conditional** or **Barter Close** (can be classified as a high- or low-risk and as a direct or indirect close, depending on usage)—The seller offers the prospect something in exchange for the buyer's

acceptance of the transaction. The word "if" normally appears as a part of this technique.

3. The **Third-Party Reference Close** (can be classified as a high- or low-risk and as a direct or indirect close, depending on usage)—The seller attempts to close the prospect by citing examples of past or present customers who are satisfied or impressed with the seller's products or services.

6

CLOSING TIPS AND TRICKS

Pitfalls of Closing and Their Causes

The mistakes salespeople most often make in relationship to closing are listed below.

Pitfall 1

The number one pitfall is that the seller does not attempt to close the prospect. This can happen for any of the following reasons:

- Fear of failure.
- Fear of closing.
- Lack of sales training.
- Lack of self-confidence.
- Limited closing repertoire.
- Fear of customer rejection.

Pitfall 2

A second pitfall is that the seller does not use trial closes. This can happen because of

- A lack of sales training.
- A lack of self-confidence.
- A lack of practice in closing.
- A lack of understanding of the importance and usage of trial closes.

Pitfall 3

Another pitfall is poor timing. The seller's closing attempts may suffer from poor timing for any of these reasons:

- Lack of planning.
- Lack of sales training.
- Lack of closing experience.

Pitfall 4

A fourth pitfall occurs when the seller lacks desire or interest in closing the prospect. This may result because of

- A lack of interest in sales.
- A lack of desire to succeed.

Pitfall 5

In pitfall number five the seller's efforts suffer from poor positioning of closing statements or questions. The seller may exhibit

- Poor listening habits.
- Lack of sales training.
- Lack of interest in sales.
- Lack of closing experience.
- Difficulty in recognizing and responding to buying signals.

Pitfall 6

A sixth pitfall results when the seller attempts to close on issues that are irrelevant to the prospect. This may happen because the seller

- Has poor listening habits.
- Cannot identify buying signals.
- Lacks a sincere interest in the customer.

Pitfall 7

Pitfall number seven occurs when the seller's poor planning practices show up in his or her sales presentations. Poor planning can be a result of

- Lack of sales training.
- Lack of common sense.
- Too much concern on the seller's part with activity and not enough time spent in thought.

Pitfall 8

In pitfall number eight the seller does not accurately identify the prospect's buying signals. Failure to identify buying signals can happen because of

- Poor listening habits.
- A lack of sales training.
- A lack of common sense.
- A lack of interest in sales.
- A lack of interest in the customer's needs.

Pitfall 9

In this final pitfall the seller fails to save the best close for the end of the closing process. This happens for one primary reason:

- Lack of forethought.

Ways to Avoid These Pitfalls

In most cases these pitfalls can be avoided with training, practice, and professional assistance from a qualified sales manager. The only situations in which this advice will not work are with those individuals who

- Do not want to sell.
- Suffer from an attitude problem.
- Do not possess a high level of common sense.
- Lack the ability to think beyond their present circumstances.
- Lack the values and drive needed to succeed in sales.

Understanding the Value of the Close

Subconsciously, most prospects decide if they like or dislike a salesperson early in the selling process. Consciously, they make that decision during the qualification step. The presentation process is rarely where they make their final buying decision because they normally make that decision earlier in the process. Rather, the presentation stage is where the customer verifies the validity of his or her conscious decision to buy or not to buy. Those buyers who are still undecided as the presentation step begins may be

- Unconvinced that the salesperson can perform as expected.
- Uncertain of the salesperson's company's ability to perform as desired.
- Unable to decide what they want or how to best satisfy their needs.

The seller must remember that the closing stage is that step in which the salesperson

- Calls for an answer.
- Requests the customer's opinion.
- Seeks an agreement with the prospect.

What Elicits a Positive or Negative Reaction from the Prospect

Table 6-1 examines how a customer's impressions are affected during the closing process. Outside the closing process, the buyer's impressions are also affected by

- The activities and communications that took place before the closing process began.
- A like or dislike of the following:

    Seller

    Seller's terms

    Seller's employer

    Seller's products or services

    Other personal biases

Table 6-1 The Anatomy of the Sale How the Prospect's Impressions Are Affected as a Result of the Closing Process	
Poor Close	Good Close
The Buyer Feels That the Seller	*The Buyer Feels That the Seller*
• Improperly assumes the customer is ready to buy. • Fails to close on relevant issues or the buyer's interests. • Fails to recognize and respond to buying signals. • Does not use closes that fit the situation. • Fails to appeal to the buyer's values and behavior. • Fails to satisfy the prospect's needs. • Closes brusquely.	• Positions and times closes for best appeal and results. • Uses a variety of soft trial closes when the buyer is ready. • Anticipates objections and answers them professionally. • Is responsive and uses body language that makes the customer comfortable. • Projects views. • Ties closes to the buyer's needs. • Is a problem solver. • Offers empathy.

The Ten Laws of Closing

The closing process is governed by a number of basic rules. When faithfully observed, these "Laws of Closing" listed in Table 6-2 will help a salesperson close more effectively.

Table 6-2 The Ten Laws of Closing
1. Never fear closing. It is your privilege, your right, and the way you earn your living.
2. Never fear rejection. It is the listener's privilege and right to reject a closing statement.
3. Position and time the closing process for maximum results. Do not close while the prospect is confused. Close when the customer is indicating that his or her needs are being met.
4. Use trial closes frequently.
5. When appropriate, position closes to follow benefit statements.
6. If the customer is closing the sale, stay out of the way (do not interrupt). Allow such buyers to talk themselves into the close.
7. If possible, avoid closing by calling for a decision. Instead, close by asking for a preference or opinion.
8. Use closing statements that appeal to the customer's needs, desires, values, and personality.
9. Respond to buying signals appropriately (for instance, replying to a question), and then always, always, always close on a buying signal.
10. Plan ahead, and save the best close for last.

Who Is Really in Control of the Sale?

Game players view their moves as offensive (implying they are actively pursuing their opponent) or defensive (protecting their position). The five steps of the sale can be viewed in the same manner.

Table 6-3 The Anatomy of the Sale Examining the Prospect's View	
Five Steps of the Sale	Prospect's View of the Seller's Role Through the Selling Process
1. Greeting	1. Offense (both parties active)
2. Warm-up	2. Offense (both parties active)
3. Qualification	3. Offense (buyer actively answers questions)
4. Presentation	4. Defense (seller active, buyer passive)
5. Close	5. Offense (buyer must make decision)

Many sellers argue that the fourth step of the sale (the presentation) is not a defensive act. They state that they are in control of the sale because they are doing all the talking. New salespeople, especially, tend to be overly focused on "taking control" of the sale. Some make the mistake of thinking that by doing most of the talking they maintain control. What they fail to understand is that by monopolizing the conversation they may well bore the prospect. If the buyer's attention is lost, the seller actually loses control of the sale.

Many prospects control the sale by encouraging the seller to do all the talking. As long as the seller is talking, the prospect is unable to say the magic words, "Yes, I want to buy." While the seller is doing all the talking, the buyer is spending time evaluating the seller and the wisdom of making a purchase. That time often allows the customer to think of questions, objections, and criticisms. The salesperson can avoid this pitfall by keeping the customer actively involved in the presentation.

A salesperson can keep the buyer's attention by

- Soliciting the customer's opinion.
- Asking the prospect leading questions.
- Showing the buyer samples or graphics.
- Encouraging the customer to participate in a demonstration.

The buyer's involvement throughout the presentation step gives that person part ownership of the process, and that is a critical aspect of making others feel important and holding their interest.

The more time the customer spends talking, the more data that person is giving the seller, and the more time the seller has to plan the sales and closing approach. Furthermore, customers like salespeople who listen to them, for listening is a form of flattery and respect.

To maintain control of the selling and closing process, a salesperson must know as much as possible about

- Customers.
- Competitors.
- Products and services.
- Psychology of selling.
- Selling, closing, and negotiating techniques.

Understanding these subjects will help the salesperson develop the confidence needed to sell and close successfully. Once the seller knows these things, guiding the customer through the sale to the close becomes easy.

Chapter Summary

1. The most common pitfalls of closing are
   - No attempt to close the prospect.
   - Failure to use trial closes.
   - Poor timing.
   - Lack of desire or interest in closing the prospect.
   - Poor positioning of closing statements or questions.
   - Attempting to close on issues irrelevant to the prospect.
   - Poor planning practices, which show up in sales presentations.
   - Not recognizing the prospect's buying signals.
   - Failure to save the best close for the end of the closing process.

2. The success of the close relies greatly on professionally executing other parts of the sale. To become an effective closer you will need to learn how to
   - Make a positive first impression.
   - Conduct a thorough qualification.
   - Time your entry into the presentation stage.
   - Conduct professional, customer-centered presentations.

3. The Ten Laws of Closing are
   - Never fear closing. It is your privilege, your right, and the way you earn your living.
   - Never fear rejection. It is the listener's privilege and right to reject a closing statement.
   - Position and time the closing process for maximum results. Do not close while the prospect is

confused. Close when the customer is indicating that his or her needs are being met.

- Use trial closes frequently.
- When appropriate, position closes to follow benefit statements.
- If the customer is closing the sale, stay out of the way (do not interrupt). Allow such buyers to talk themselves into the close.
- If possible, avoid closing by calling for a decision. Instead, close by asking for a preference or opinion.
- Use closing statements that appeal to the customer's needs, desires, values, and personality.
- Respond to buying signals appropriately (for instance, replying to a question), and then always, always, always close on a buying signal.
- Plan ahead, and save the best close for last.

4. When you are talking, your buyer is spending time thinking. That time often allows the customer to think of questions, objections, and criticisms that may not have occurred earlier. You can avoid this pitfall by keeping your customer actively involved in your presentation by

- Soliciting the buyer's opinion.
- Asking the prospect leading questions.
- Showing the customer samples or graphics.
- Encouraging the buyer to participate in a demonstration.

THE NEXT STEP

The pragmatist understands that selling is more than just getting something from someone else. Selling is a sharing process in which all are given the opportunity to satisfy their needs.

Many salespeople overemphasize the importance of the close. These people speak of the close as if it were the only purpose for a sales call. Ironically, buyers themselves see the close much differently. They see the close as a natural outgrowth of the selling process, assuming everything else (especially the qualification and presentation stages) was handled professionally.

How important is the close? Since it relies so greatly on the third step for direction of the sale, the close is second to the qualification step in importance. Over ninety percent of closing mistakes I have observed occurred as a result of errors and poor assumptions by the seller during the qualification step. For sellers who regularly botch the third step of the sale, it should be retitled the *misqualification step*.

Some salespeople are employed as professional closers. They normally have no other responsibility than to close. They rely greatly on their fellow salespeople who are trained to handle the first four steps of the sale. One of the steps is qualification, and the salesperson must inform the closer that the buyer's needs were uncovered during that step. Good qualifications lead to solid presentations and positive closing situations. Poor qualifications mislead sellers into making presentations that are of no interest to the prospect, and cause the seller to make inappropriate closes.

Selling is more than just getting something from someone else. So is closing. There is a give-and-take process that occurs during the sale. This process includes

- The determination of whether or not the buyer and seller like each other.
- The determination of whether or not the buyer and seller respect each other.
- The determination of whether or not the buyer and seller trust each other.
- The determination of how much information the buyer and seller will share with each other.
- The determination of whether or not the buyer and seller will conduct business with each other.

The close relies on the success of many other practices. It is surprising to see that many salespeople are concerned with learning how to close before they learn how to avoid

1. Making poor first impressions on their customers.
2. Rushing to the presentation stage.
3. Appearing to be a *pusher of products.*

The next step beyond this book is simply to practice what you have learned about closing.

And, in all that you have learned and will continue to learn about selling, remember

The pragmatist understands that selling is more than just getting something from someone else. Selling is a sharing process in which all are given the opportunity to satisfy their needs.

THE COMPENDIUM OF CLOSES

Experienced salespeople know that possessing a variety of closes is critical to their selling success.

The following closes and implied closes are listed alphabetically by classification. The subtle rephrasing of a close can change its classification; therefore, many of the statements and questions that follow are combinations and variations of other closes. With a little forethought and care, these closes can be altered to fit any type of sales, negotiation, or personal communication situation.

Some of these phrases are actual closing statements or questions, while other phrases lead into the close. A listing in this section is neither an endorsement nor a recommendation of the close. Rather, select those closes that best fit

- Your selling style.
- Your selling situation.
- Your product or service.
- Your customer's personality.
- Your organization's image, objectives, and policies.

The Add-On Close

"This is such a good buy, why not pick up a second model as well?"

"Then we'll ship your request right away. What else would you like to order today?"

"If you buy another unit, you'll receive a third one free of charge. Should I write it up?"

"This suit really looks good on you. How about buying a new tie that will complement it?"

"Now that you've purchased the basic units, do you want to purchase the accessories we discussed?"

"If you increase your order, I can discount your purchase by ten percent. How many more units would you like?"

"You've just made a good investment. Now would you like to protect that investment with an extended service policy?"

"Thank you for your order. Now would you like to protect the finish on your unit by allowing us to coat it with a protective glaze?"

"You'll enjoy this system for years to come. This would be a wise time to add the component we were looking at earlier, wouldn't it?"

"If your organization buys an extended service policy now, I can offer you a twenty-five percent savings. Should I write the agreement to cover this purchase or make it retroactive to protect your past purchases as well?"

The Asking for the Order Close

"Do you want to buy one?"

"Can I write this up for you?"

"Should I wrap this up for you?"

"Is there anything else you want?"

"Can we do business on this now?"

"Shall I sell you one of these today?"

"Should I send this out to you today?"

"Can we count on an order from you?"

"Should I begin processing your order?"

"Will your organization buy our concept?"

"Would you like an extended service policy?"

"Have you made a decision to buy this one?"

"Is this model the one you want me to write up?"

"Can your company issue a purchase order number now?"

The Assumptive Close

"Let's write up the order."

"You'll like it. You'll see."

"Then let's get started on it."

"How many would you like?"

"You wanted two cases, right?"

"I'll get going on it right away!"

"When do you want it delivered?"

"We'll wrap that one up for you."

"You're charging this, I suppose?"

"Then expect our truck on Monday."

"Tomorrow is a good delivery day, right?"

"Then you probably want the larger model?"

"Did you say Friday was a good delivery day?"

"This is a smart buy. You'll be glad you made it."

"Are we in agreement as to the size of your order?"

"I'll get the four dozen to you as soon as possible."

"We'll invoice you sometime in the next two weeks."

"Then we are in agreement as to the size of your order."

"Excellent. I'll make that notation on your sales request."

"I'll put in your association's request for this order today."

"Use our samples for a week. I'll get back to you regarding the terms."

"Let's write up a request and get our operations people moving on this."

"I'll assign your order a number and you can expect a Monday delivery."

"I'm sure your boss (spouse) will like your purchase. I'll get it ready for you."

"Now I'm sure you'll want an extended service contract to protect your investment."

"Please let your boss (spouse) know that we'll start working on your order tomorrow."

"Good, then you'll arrange a meeting for us with your purchasing committee. What day is best for you?"

"You are going to have to make this investment sometime. The only remaining question is, do you want to pay for it now or later?"

The Backup or Alternate Vendor Close

"As a backup vendor for your organization, all we're asking for is our fair share of your business. Doesn't that sound reasonable to you?"

"Employing a backup vendor is like having an insurance policy in which you receive real goods and services. In other words, you get the insurance aspects of the relationship at no expense to you or your organization. You agree that it's a win-win situation for all concerned, don't you?"

"I appreciate that your present vendor is doing a good job for your association. You should have a backup supplier in case that company increases its prices. Don't you think a relationship with a backup vendor would be a smart move for you and your organization?"

"No doubt you have a good supplier. Have you considered what benefits you may be losing with only one vendor servicing your account? An occasional purchase from us may cause your present supplier to work harder for you. Why don't you give us an opportunity to supply you for ninety days?"

The Choice Close
(*see also* The Preference Close)

"Did you say you needed four or five boxes?"

"Are you considering using your credit card or cash?"

"Do you want this service for a twelve- or twenty-four-month period?"

"Can you afford to wait, or would you prefer to act now?"

"Is your company going to pay for it now or on delivery?"

"Can we count on your full order this week or next week?"

"Do you want me to enter your request on Monday or Tuesday?"

"When is a better time to start the program, Thursday or Friday?"

"Will your company want this model or the more advanced one?"

"Do you want to pick it up, or do you want us to deliver it to you?"

"Were you considering a lay-away program or purchasing it today?"

"Would you like the payments to fall on the first or the middle of the month?"

"That item is an excellent choice. Do you want to make a deposit or pay for it in full?"

"Did you want to keep that model or do you want us to deliver a new one next month?"

"Is this what you want, or were you thinking of adding a unit or two more to your order?"

"Would you like to buy the entire set tonight or purchase one item a month for the next twelve months?"

"Do you want me to demonstrate the product at this time, or do you want your boss (spouse) to also see the demonstration?"

"Would you like your purchasing committee to see our products in a live demonstration or view that demonstration by videotape?"

"Do you want your superiors to decide without seeing the working model, or would you rather I make a full presentation to them?"

The Conditional or Barter Close

"If we lower our price, will your association give us a full order?"

"Will you give us all of your business if we meet all your conditions?"

"If I show you a way of saving money using this service, will you buy it?"

"Will you place an order with us if your boss approves of this transaction?"

"If I show you a way to save money with this plan, will you review it with me?"

"If we can improve our delivery time, will you consider giving us a larger order?"

"Will you allow me to meet with your boss if I demonstrate how my actions will benefit you?"

"If I can assure you that you'll be completely reimbursed should any damage occur, would you again review our proposal?"

"If I show you how this move will help you and your organization, will you allow me to talk with your purchasing committee?"

"If I show you a way of saving money using our services, would you be interested in listening to how it could put money into your pocket?"

The Financial Balance Sheet Close

"Let's evaluate the financial pros and cons of this purchase."

"Let's take a look at how we could save you money through our special sale."

"Let's compare your present costs with the kind of savings you can expect from our program."

"Let's estimate your investment in buying this service now versus what you might pay if you don't make the right investment now."

"Let's compare the investment you'll make in our products, item by item, against what the other vendor wants you to pay."

"Let's compare the amount of time and the resulting costs involved that your organization invests in your present systems. Then let's compare that time and cost factor with what our program will save you."

The Five Yeses Close

Example 1

"Our price does fit in your budget, doesn't it?"

"You compared our service against others, right?"

"You would like to start the program tomorrow, right?"

"You did say it's the best program you've seen, correct?"

"You did say that you need the benefits of this program, didn't you?"

Example 2

"This is the color you wanted, right?"

"This is the model you wanted, isn't it?"

"This is the size you wanted, am I correct?"

"Sounds like you've made up your mind, doesn't it?"

"Did you say that our financing terms are satisfactory?"

The Guilt Close

"Doesn't your family deserve the better model?"

"Don't you want your organization and peers to succeed?"

"Isn't your health more important than making this small purchase?"

"You mean you would deprive your family of these benefits?"

"Isn't your peace of mind important enough to finalize your decision today?"

"After all the work you've put into this project, don't you deserve to treat yourself to this purchase?"

"Don't you think you should care more about yourself and less about how much money you're spending?"

"What's the value of all the effort you've put into your work if you can't enjoy your money through a program like this one?"

"I've been your sales representative for nearly a year now. How could you turn your back on such a positive working relationship?"

The Higher Reference Close

"Your boss suggested that you consider our products and services."

"Your boss really likes this program. Shouldn't you at least spend a few minutes reviewing it?"

"Your manager uses our services and thought that you might like to evaluate our program for your use as well."

"Your executive committee is very much in favor of this proposal. Wouldn't it be a good idea to work in accordance with their feelings?"

"Your manager used our services in the past and was very satisfied with the results. Would you be interested in reviewing what impressed your boss about our program?"

The Intimidation Close

"The price is going up tomorrow. Better buy now!"

"It's our last one. If you want it, better make your decision immediately!"

"You may lose whatever advantage you have going for you if you don't act today."

"If you don't act now, there may not be any opportunity to deliver your item on time."

"Why put yourself through more stress. Why not make the right decision and buy now?"

"What would you say to your boss if she or he discovers that you turned down a free offer from us?"

"What will you do if you encounter a costly repair and you're without a service contract?"

"If we don't write up something today, I can't guarantee that you will receive a discount."

"Why allow your competitors to get the drop on you? Why not get the edge on them by buying now?"

"Just to be on the safe side, shouldn't you protect your company's purchase with an extended service policy?"

"You know your boss won't like it if this ends up costing your company more, when you can act now and save yourself the risk."

"This is an opportune moment for you to act on this matter. If you fail to do so, your peers may take advantage of this mistake."

"You can't afford to make a decision without seeing a service that might save you nearly fifty percent over your present suppliers, can you?"

"Who will be held responsible for not allowing us to meet with your purchasing committee? Why don't we play it safe and talk with them?"

"Why not shift the responsibility of making the purchasing decision to a team level and allow us to make a presentation to you and your boss (spouse)?"

"Do you want your boss to make this decision without the benefit of my input, or would you rather I protect both of you by my making a full presentation?"

"Your purchasing committee wouldn't like hearing that you turned down a vendor who is offering your organization a better product at a lower price, would it?"

"If you act now on our trial offer, you will save nearly fifty percent over our regular price! If you fail to act, you will pay double the rate for the same service. Which would you prefer?"

"If something happens to you or your family during this period, it will cost you a lot of money. Why don't you act today and enjoy the peace of mind this purchase will bring you?"

"While you may save money temporarily by purchasing that lower cost item, think of your long-term grief and expense when it starts breaking down. Don't you think it would be wiser and less expensive to invest in a better product such as ours to begin with?"

The Loaded Yes Close

"This is the color you ordered, isn't it?"

"This is the model you wanted, isn't it?"

"Our price sounds reasonable, doesn't it?"

"You do want to buy this today, don't you?"

"This is what your boss (spouse) ordered, isn't it?"

"You do want a model that fits all of your needs, don't you?"

"You did say that you wanted a time-saving system, didn't you?"

"You did say this would look beautiful in your home, didn't you?"

"You do want to make a purchase that is cost-effective, don't you?"

"This does fit your purchasing committee's requirements, doesn't it?"

"You did say that you wanted the best model available, didn't you?"

"You do want a unit that makes your boss (spouse) happy, don't you?"

"You do want a system that covers all your organization's needs, don't you?"

"You did say that this item was exactly what you were looking for, didn't you?"

"Your boss (spouse) is interested in buying a product that solves the problem, isn't he?"

The Minor Point Close

"Is there another color you prefer?"

"This is the style you want, isn't it?"

"Our price sounds reasonable, doesn't it?"

"You do want to buy this today, don't you?"

"Did you say Friday was a good delivery day?"

"Do you think the larger unit would fit in your room?"

"Wouldn't you like one of these impressive units in your office?"

"Your boss wouldn't care about such a small purchase, would she?"

"You are authorized to approve a purchase of this size, are you not?"

"At this late date, this isn't the time to make changes in your order, is it?"

"Your purchasing committee would approve an order of this size, wouldn't it?"

"No one would question your buying an extended service contract, would they?"

"Have you considered what financial terms your company will be interested in?"

"Would you like our service people to check the system in our service facility or at your location?"

The Misstated Higher Quantity Close

"Did you say you needed four or forty?" (When the prospect was interested in the lower number.)

"You did say that you wanted 4,050 units, didn't you?" (When the prospect originally indicated a smaller number.)

The Pity Close

"I'm just like you; all I'm trying to do is earn a living. Can't we do business on this item?"

"All we're asking for is our fair share of your business. Doesn't that sound reasonable to you?"

"Quite frankly, my job is on the line. If I don't bring in one more order today, I may not have a job tomorrow. Can't you see your way clear to give me just one more order?"

"You know, we're more than just business acquaintances; we're friends. You can't do this to a friend. You have my promise as a friend that your order will be processed immediately!"

The Preference Close
(*see also* The Choice Close)

"What other day would you prefer?"

"What would you prefer instead of this one?"

"Would you prefer one of our other models?"

"Do you prefer a Friday or Monday delivery?"

"Do you prefer taking care of this by check or cash?"

"Would you prefer a morning or afternoon delivery?"

"Would you prefer our invoicing you or charging it?"

"Would you prefer starting the service in May or June?"

"Is there another color you prefer, such as this lighter one?"

"Would you prefer a one-year or a five-year maintenance policy?"

"Would your company prefer a demonstration in our factory or in yours?"

"Do you want to install it, or do you want one of our people to install it for you?"

"Would your association prefer to contact your membership or have us contact them?"

"Would you prefer that our service people perform the maintenance, or would you rather we train your service people to complete the same operation?"

The Puppy Dog Close

"Why don't you try our product free of charge for a week?"

"Why don't you test one of our models for the next thirty days and see if it meets your needs?"

"Try our product in your home or office for the next three weeks. If you like it, keep it, and we'll invoice you later."

"Use our service for the next five days free of charge. If you like it, we'll begin invoicing during the second week. That's more than fair, isn't it?"

The Reverse Psychology Close

"You mean you would deprive your family of these benefits?"

"You're probably not interested in a money-back guarantee, are you?"

"You're probably not interested in an interest-free charge system, are you?"

"You're probably not interested in a money-saving plan like this one, are you?"

"You're probably not interested in all these extra features at no added cost to you, are you?"

"Your boss probably wouldn't be too angry with you if you made the wrong decision, would he?"

"Your organization probably isn't interested in the same quality service/product for a lower price, correct?"

"Your family probably wouldn't be interested in something that can save them time, like this unit can, right?"

"You probably weren't thinking about a program that would pay for itself within the next ninety days, were you?"

"Your purchasing committee probably wouldn't want to deal with a vendor who could save you both time and money, would it?"

"Your organization is so profitable, it probably wouldn't be interested in reviewing a program that could increase its profits, would it?"

"You probably wouldn't get in trouble with your boss if you failed to set up a meeting with a vendor who could improve your organization's output at no added cost, would you?"

The Third-Party Reference Close

"Wouldn't you want the same model your friends use?"

"According to the rating council, this is the best and safest unit available. Shouldn't you have the best?"

"The leading companies in your industry buy from us. Shouldn't you at least look at our product line?"

"According to all the magazines, this is the most fashionable model available. Don't you want to be in style?"

"Four of your neighbors bought units from me last night. Wouldn't you like to fit in with the neighborhood?"

"With the top associations now using our services, shouldn't your purchasing committee at least talk with one of our representatives?"

The Trial-Offer Close

"Why don't you try our service free of charge for a week as a way of evaluating our efficiency?"

"If you act now on our trial offer, you will save nearly fifty percent over our regular price! Would you prefer three or four of these items?"

The Trial-Order Close

"If you sample our products through our trial-order program, you pay for the initial order only if we meet your standards."

"Try our service for the next ten weeks. If our service isn't more cost-effective than your present suppliers, cancel our agreement."

"Let's start you on our program with a small trial order. Evaluate our products and services without risking a large order. Isn't that fair?"

"Why don't you use our products on a trial basis for thirty days. If you like them, send us a check for the amount listed on our trial-agreement form. If for any reason you don't like them, send them back any time during the trial period and there's no charge to you."

The Weighing or Ben Franklin Close

"Let's evaluate the pros and cons of this decision."

"Do you have a sheet of paper so that we can evaluate this challenge logically? Please list all the reasons you feel this may be a less-than-desirable move on the left side of the paper. Then let's list all the reasons why you should make this move on the right side."

GLOSSARY

A

Action. Fourth of the four elements of a sale in which the seller attempts to close the prospect. See also *AIDA*.

AIDA. The four elements of a sale. AIDA outlines what the seller must accomplish during the face-to-face sale. AIDA is an acronym for

- A: *Attention*—the stage in which the seller captures the prospect's attention.
- I: *Interest*—the stage in which the seller develops the prospect's interest.
- D: *Desire*—the stage in which the seller builds the prospect's desire.
- A: *Action*—the stage in which the seller gets the action (commitment) desired of the prospect.

The theoretical flow of the selling process. A technique also used in all forms of advertising (radio, television, billboard, direct mail, print), public relations, and public speaking. One of eight major areas that sales managers use to assess a salesperson's abilities. See also *Action, Anatomy of the Sale, Attention, Desire, Interest*.

Anatomy of the Sale. An overview of the dynamics of the selling process and how they relate to each other. For example:

Four Elements	Five Steps
What sellers want from their customers or prospects	*How sellers go about achieving their objectives*
1. Attention ⟶	1. Greeting
1. Attention and 2. Interest ⟶	2. Warm-up
2. Interest ⟶	3. Qualification
3. Desire ⟶	4. Presentation
4. Action ⟶	5. Close

See also *Action, AIDA, Attention, Desire, Five Steps of the Sale, Interest.*

Attention. First of the four elements of the sale in which the salesperson attempts to capture the buyer's attention by discussing issues that are of interest to that person. See also AIDA.

B

Basic Steps of the Sale. See *Five Steps of the Sale.*

Buying Decision. The decision to make a purchase. What the seller attempts to obtain from the buyer during the closing process. See also *Buying Decision Maker, Buying Decision Process, Close.*

Buying Decision Maker. The individual who has the authority to make a purchase and makes that decision. See also *Buying Decision, Buying Decision Process.*

Buying Decision Process. The way a buyer goes about determining how to make a purchase, including those relevant players who are involved in the process. See also *Buying Decision.*

Buying Signal. Any indication by prospects that they are ready to buy.

C

Close. A point of agreement. Step of the sale in which the salesperson finalizes an agreement (close) between himself or herself and the buyer; for example, agreeing to

- A future appointment.
- Actual purchase of a product or service.
- Disbursement of monies owed the vendor.
- Allowing seller to make a presentation or demonstration.
- Allowing seller to gather data vital to the sales presentation.
- Meeting with the decision maker or purchasing committee or other interested parties.
- Consideration as a vendor or alternate vendor (placement on the approved vendor's list).
- Selling and buying terms—size, price, color, flavor, quality, quantity, delivery day, financing option.
- Agreement dealing with some other service- or product-related issue.
- Extending the salesperson special privileges other than those mentioned thus far.

The close is the fifth and final step of the sales transaction. A close is also a negotiating ploy. It is one of eight major areas that sales managers use to assess a salesperson's abilities. Depending on its use, this tactic can be classified as a low- or high-risk negotiating technique. See also *Anatomy of the Sale, Closing Classifications*.

Closing Classifications. Various ways to reach an agreement during a communication, sale, or some other negotiation, such as:

- Add-on Close
- Alternate or Backup Vendor Close
- Asking for the Order Close
- Assumptive Close
- Choice Close
- Conditional or Barter Close
- Financial Balance Sheet Close
- Five Yeses Close
- Guilt Close
- Higher Reference Close
- Intimidation Close
- Loaded Yes Close
- Minor Point Close
- Misstated Higher Quantity Close
- Pity Close
- Preference Close
- Puppy Dog Close
- Reverse Psychology Close
- Self Close
- Third-Party Reference Close
- Trial-Offer Close
- Trial-Order Close
- Weighing or Ben Franklin Close

See also *Close*.

Commitment. Dedication to an activity or person.

Commitment Statement. A statement of agreement. A positive response to a statement or question posed by the salesperson. A verbal or written commitment by the customer indicating that he or she is interested in or willing to make a purchase.

D

Decision Maker. The person having the responsibility and authority to make the final decision on a matter.

Desire. A wish or nonessential want. That which a person or group may want but does not need. One of ten factors that motivates a buyer to make a purchase. The third element of the selling process of AIDA, in which the seller tries to entice the buyer into making a purchase. See also *AIDA*.

Direct Close. A high-risk communication technique a seller uses to elicit a positive buying decision from a prospect. An aggressive statement or question that tests the prospect's buying readiness. The use of an overt question or statement to bring completion or agreement to an issue.

F

Five Steps of the Sale. A logical approach to verbal sales communications.

The five steps consist of the

1. Greeting
2. Warm-up
3. Qualification
4. Presentation
5. Close

See also *Anatomy of the Sale, Close, Greeting, Presentation, Qualification, Warm-up.*

Four Elements of the Sale. Theoretical foundation on which the selling process is built. What the seller wants to accomplish. See also *AIDA.*

G

Greeting. The first step of a sale in which the salesperson meets the buyer and introduces himself or herself; the step that sets the tone for the transaction. See also *Anatomy of the Sale, Five Steps of the Sale.*

H

High-Risk Close. A close that may threaten the listener. A closing technique that may endanger the closing process. A closer's overt use of slurs, force, innuendos, aggressive statements, or pressure-oriented questions intended to drive the listener into making a decision favorable to the closer.

I

Indirect Close. A nonaggressive or subtle statement or question that tests the prospect's buying readiness.

Interest. The second element of the selling process of AIDA, in which the salesperson stimulates the buyer's interest in the vendor's presentation, goods, and services. See also *AIDA.*

L

Low-Risk Close. Statements and questions a seller uses to elicit positive responses from a prospect.

P

Presentation. The fourth step of the sale; the demonstration or discussion of a product or service during which the salesperson gives the buyer enough data to make a positive buying decision. Also used in reference to

- One's appearance.
- The appearance of a product or brochure.
- The entire time a seller spends with a prospect.

See also *Anatomy of the Sale, Five Steps of the Sale.*

Problem Solver. A person who tries to

- Fill the prospect's needs.
- Meet the prospect's challenges.
- Answer the customer's problems.

See also *Problem Solving.*

Problem Solving. The art of reaching a solution or conclusion to some need, challenge, or problem. See also *Problem Solver.*

Q

Qualification. The practice of determining another's needs or position by asking questions or offering probing statements. The third step of the sale in which the salesperson asks questions (known as the Six W's) to determine the listener's legitimacy as a prospect. See also *Anatomy of the Sale, Five Steps of the Sale, Six Ws.*

S

Sales. A function of marketing. A form of communicating with others. The amount sold (normally expressed in

financial terms or in units). The act of bartering and negotiating products or services for something of value.

Salesperson. One who negotiates and barters products,
services, or money for something of value. Also referred
to as: Account Executive, Account Manager, Account
Representative, Agent, Canvasser, Clerk, Counterjum-
per, Counterperson, Door Knocker, Door-to-Door Salesperson, Drummer, Fieldperson, Field Rep, Field
Salesperson, Hawker, Huckster, Inside Rep, Inside Salesperson, National Account Manager, National Account
Salesperson, Peddler, Sales Consultant, Sales Engineer,
Salesgirl, Saleslady, Salesman, Sales Rep, Saleswoman,
Seller, Selling Agent, Shopgirl, Shopman, Solicitor, Travel-
ing Salesman, Vendor. See also *Sales.*

Selling Steps. See *Five Steps of a Sale.*

Six Ws. Six types of questions a salesperson must ask a
buyer during the qualification stage of a sale. The gathering
of information the seller needs to tailor his or her presentation to the buyer's needs. Questions that encourage customers to reveal their needs and agenda. The Six Ws are

- Who
- What
- Where
- When
- Why
- HoW

Steps of the Sale. See *Five Steps of a Sale.*

T

Trial Close. A subtle approach testing a prospect's readiness to buy.

W

Warm-up. The second step in the sales process in which the seller's objectives are to

- Encourage the buyer to relax.
- Become accustomed to the environment.
- Establish a rapport with the buyer by discussing issues of interest to that person.

Casual conversation dealing with topics the buyer

- Relates with.
- Enjoys talking about.
- Feels are nonthreatening.
- Responds to in a positive way.

See also *Anatomy of the Sale, Five Steps of the Sale.*

ABOUT THE AUTHOR

Andoni Lizardy, president of Lizardy Associates, is a management consultant, speaker, and author of twelve business books and courses that deal with sales, sales management, sales planning, negotiations, customer relations, communications, business psychology, and time management. He is also a salesperson who sells products and services both nationally and internationally.

He has trained tens of thousands of sales, marketing, and customer service people as well as sales and general managers. Since developing courses for the world's largest management association, over half of the top Fortune 500 companies have sent people to his seminars while a number of American, Asian, and European companies employ him as a consultant.

As a much sought after keynote speaker, he lectures internationally in London, Zurich, Athens, Cairo, Singapore, Hong Kong, Tokyo, Edmonton, and Toronto, for a wide variety of associations and business organizations.

Andoni Lizardy has also lectured at Kent State University and has guest lectured at the University of Toronto, the University of Pittsburgh, and the University of Pennsylvania's Wharton School of Business. When not working with his clients, he spends his time between offices in San Diego and Santa Barbara, California.

INDEX